# THREE TIMES SOLD

# THREE TIMES SOLD

## *A Story of Faith, Survival and Freedom*

## Sioni Rodriguez

ISBN: 1978222742
ISBN-13: 978-1978222748

I have tried to recreate events, locales and conversations from my memories of
them. In order to maintain their anonymity in some instances I have changed
the names of individuals and places, I may have changed some identifying
characteristics and details such as physical properties, and places of residence.

Scriptures taken from the Holy Bible, New International Version®, NIV®.
Copyright © 1973, 1978, 1984, 2011
by Biblica, Inc.™ Used by permission of Zondervan. All rights reserved
worldwide. www.zondervan.com. The "NIV" and "New International Version"
are trademarks registered in the United States Patent and Trademark Office by
Biblica, Inc.™

writer-editor, Jane Fisher
www.janefisheronline.com

Printed in the United States of America

Available for purchase at Amazon.com

# DEDICATION

To my Lord Jesus Christ
Whom I love, serve and give praise.

To my children
Scheila and Cheo, the joys of my life,
of whom I am so proud.

To my grandchildren
We cherish you, our hope and our future.

To my husband, Richard
Thank you for loving me enough
to spend your life with me.

*Los quiero mucho.*

*For I am convinced that neither death nor life, neither angels nor demons, neither the present nor the future, nor any powers, neither height nor depth, nor anything else in all creation, will be able to separate us from the love of God that is in Christ Jesus our Lord.*

**Romans 8:38–39**

# CONTENTS

# CONTENTS

# CONTENTS

ABOUT THE AUTHOR

# CONTENTS

# FOREWORD

It was our regular weekly call. Sioni had been telling me stories about her life, and I'd been compiling them into her book for the last two months.

"Jane." I waited for her to tell me whatever was on her mind. "I couldn't sleep last night. I finally got up to pray—I felt like God had something to say to me. It was the weirdest thing, though. I kept getting a list of words. I don't know why, but I couldn't get this list out of my head. I wrote them down."

"That's fine, Sioni. Go ahead and give me the list." I copied it down.

| | | |
|---|---|---|
| *overcome* | *victory* | *mistakes* |
| *open wound* | *reaching the goal* | *life's promise* |
| *faith* | *thankful* | *forgiveness* |
| *blessing* | *love, love, love* | *rejection* |
| *confidence* | *let go* | *God is my help* |
| *fear* | *belief* | *running the race* |
| *peace in God* | *challenges* | *discouraged* |
| *protected by God* | *tough decisions* | *peace in my mind* |
| *rejoice* | *love for me* | *future* |
| *trust* | *failure* | *hopeless* |

"What do you think it means?" she asked.

"I don't know, but I'm going to save this list for you. If it's got a purpose, it'll make itself known."

It wasn't until weeks later that we figured it out. I was piecing together the first draft, and starting to think about what the book would look like. Would I use a simple number for each chapter? Or give each chapter a name?

Then I remembered the list. I counted the number of chapters I had. That worked. So far, so good. Then I tried matching the words and phrases to each chapter's essence. The first 22 chapters effectively chose their own names quite easily. The next five took a full read to discern the connection. I almost couldn't bear to look at the last three. What if they didn't match? Would I change the focus of the chapter to match the remaining three names? Would I change some of what she listed? Would I find out how silly it was for me to think that all 30 would fit without any planning?

But they fit.

# FOREWORD

I should've expected it. If Sioni is "getting a word," I listen. She just seems to know.

One of my first questions to Sioni was to ask what the purpose of her book would be. Her answer was immediate and sure. "I want to give hope to others who have been abused as I was. I want to teach that forgiveness is a gift you give yourself. I want to give away what was taken from me, to release my burdens. And I want to speak Life to people everywhere."

She must have been gifted with the capacity to forgive by God before she was born. She comes to forgiveness naturally – not from a place of weakness. Quite the opposite, she forgives from her inherent strength of conviction. Sioni understands that anger and bitterness are burdens, too heavy to bear.

It has been my honor and privilege to assist on this project. Sioni's faith in God, her love of family, and her willingness to give are unsurpassed. I am grateful to be a witness to her ministry.

*Jane Fisher*

# PREFACE

We're walking to the Chinese Lantern Festival in Franklin Square. It's the middle of May, and although the sun is shining, the breeze in Philadelphia today is somewhat cool.

Richard is carrying our little grandson, holding him protectively against his chest. I am walking with our granddaughter.

"Abuela? Please don't forget that you said I could have Cheetos," she reminds me, her brow furrowed.

"No, Xianni," I reply, matching her serious tone. "I would never forget that!"

Behind us, my children and their spouses are happily chattering away. Everyone is laughing and talking at the same time. The girls only met last night, but to my joy, seem to have become family at once. My son and his wife are visiting from Texas and we're having a family lunch. It's the first time my daughter and her husband have seen their little nephew, Sergio, and met my son's wife. It's the first time ever that we've all been together in one place.

Everyone is excited and happy at the chance for this family reunion and we're all eager to hear each other's stories. We're finally seated and the little ones settled. I look around the table at my beautiful family, and my heart is full to overflowing. A wonderful peace settles over me. I know that as hard, awful, terrible as the first half of my life was, living through it all has brought me here to this place. Finally, I am completely surrounded by love!

So many memories begin to fill my mind. I see clearly, my son, Cheo, as a small boy hoarding his tiny toy treasures in his little pockets. Then, here he is now, a graduate of West Point. I can hear Scheila, as a little girl, laughing as she watched *I Love Lucy* on TV. Before long, she is serving in the Army, and then working towards her master's degree. I recall meeting Richard, the man who would become my husband. Somehow, I knew I could trust him, and he made me feel protected. He still does.

Along with these wonderful memories, others not so wonderful are swimming in my head. I remember Costa Rica, my mother, father, brothers, my first marriage, all the hurt, abuse, pain, and ugliness.

I see myself—a small, dark-haired, 12-year-old girl. By then, I had suffered enough for several lifetimes. Still, I accepted Jesus as my Savior. And when I accepted Him, *like a light coming on*, came the sure knowledge that somehow, sometime, someway, God would lead me to peace.

Yet there were still many years to come in my life, even in my Christian life, that were very unhappy. I think of the many times I was dealing with difficult issues, some emotional and some financial. Sometimes those things affected my mood, my attitude and my ability to see the positive in my life. But the more I believed in God, and hoped in God, the stronger I became. The more I trusted God, life began to change in small and wonderful ways.

I remember meeting a lovely woman at church, a stranger, put in my path for a purpose. I remember feeling light and free when, through God's Grace, I was able to forgive those who had hurt me so badly. I remember finding a job when I needed it. But most of all, I remember finally experiencing the complete absence of fear.

And as I look at my family, I know this Biblical truth: *Everything has a purpose.*

I know there are many women—and men too—who are victimized and suffering, as I was; feeling hopeless and alone, as I did.

I want them to know for certain that we can have hope, we can have strength, and we can have a better future. When we trust in God, when we allow the Holy Spirit of God to come into our lives, He makes all things possible. He dwells within us forever, and He will never leave or forsake us. What a cause for joy and comfort!

*Sioni Rodriguez*

# ACKNOWLEDGEMENTS

There are several people who have helped me throughout the writing of this book. This project would still be a vague idea without you!

Thank you to Pastor Scott Carver, of Pleasant Valley Assembly of God in Brodheadsville, PA. From the first day we met, I've felt your unwavering support and encouragement. Thanks for always being in my corner and cheering me on! You are a great blessing to our congregation and to all who know you.

Thanks to Kelly Carver, my good friend and the sister of my heart. You have always been at my side, ready to listen and encourage. How I love your kindness and sincerity. I thank you for your enthusiasm, your moral support, and your love.

Thank you, Frances Keeler, for helping to make a dream come true. And thank you for all the walks we took to discuss this book. You helped me to find the emotions that have been buried inside me for so long. I

# ACKNOWLEDGEMENTS

thank God for bringing you into my life. You will always be in my heart.

And of course, many heartfelt thanks to Jane. Thank you for seeing the possibilities and accepting the challenge. Thank you for understanding the purpose and connecting with it. I appreciate all the phone calls, the questions, the brainstorming time, and hard work.

And to my husband, Richard, thank you for giving me the confidence to believe that my story could, and should, be told. You assured me that we all have a history and that telling mine might help others. I am truly thankful that you're in my life.

And with my whole being, I thank God. The writing of this book has brought me to realize again just how essential He is to my life.

# *Open Wound*

My childhood might have destroyed me. But it didn't. I could have grown to be a bitter and lost woman. But I haven't. I haven't because God has been with me through it all!

I need to tell this story because I want to be a champion for others who were abused, as I was. So that *they* will not be destroyed, or bitter, or lost.

I feel so much compassion for anyone who is suffering, whether physically or emotionally. I want to reach out to them to share the fullness of God's love and the hope that it brings.

The beginning of my story is very hard to tell. The memories of my childhood, buried for so long, have been difficult to untangle from each other. Some things in my youngest years are cruelly unblurred. Others, when I should have been able to remember more, have been suppressed so that it takes the telling of the story for the memories to become evident.

Sometimes my story jumps out of sequence, with another memory taking precedence over the first so that I can think of nothing else.

I believe this story unfolds as it was meant to—in a way that others who were also subjected to cruel, inhumane treatment will understand.

It's the end of my story that stands indisputably clear to me. My life could have been consumed in pain, leaving a gaping, open wound.

Instead, God protected me from permanent damage. God's promise that He has more planned for me than a life of pain, has kept me hopeful and forward-looking.

Instead of being wounded, I've been healed.

# *Challenges*

Mumbai today is a cosmopolitan, bustling city. It is home to movie makers and pop stars. It is familiar with and part of modern life.

But when I was born there in 1970, it was not so forward-thinking and accepting, particularly where unwed mothers were concerned. The treatment of women in that situation was very harsh. Even more so harsh if the father was an absent non-Indian. That is the environment where I began my life.

My mother's family found out she was pregnant after she had a near-accident. Even at a young age, she had to help with the animals. She was milking a cow when it happened. The cow knocked the milk bucket over, spilling its contents. She wasn't showing yet. But my mother tried to avoid being kicked in the stomach by the cow. That's when her family discovered that she was pregnant.

She was turned out, disowned and left with her unborn child to fend for herself. Thinking about it, this is likely the reason that she was so filled with anger and rage.

The result is that she was emotionally crippled; unable to show or feel love or affection. Was she withholding from us the love and support she never received herself? Was her violence directed at us, her own children? Or at her family in India? Maybe it's as simple as her blaming us for the loss of her family. Whatever it was, she punished us continually for it.

I don't know much about my mother's family. In fact, I know nothing about them. She never spoke of her parents or extended family. Once they disowned her, they seemed to cease to exist for her.

# Challenges

I was the second child of this poor, unwed Indian woman and an absent Costa Rican father. Their first child together was a son, one year older than me.

We lived in a suburb of Bombay. We were most definitely not in the city. It was more of a shanty town than a suburb, filled with hovels, poverty and miserable living.

What I remember most from those early years was the mud. There were no paved roads or streets, and what you might call a road was packed down dirt. When it rained, everything and everywhere was mud. As all poor children do, my brother and I found fun wherever we could, making a playground of the deep mud puddles.

My father did not live with us in India, and to my knowledge, he made no contribution to our support. I don't know how my mother managed. Later events in my life pointed to what may have been her means of making an income.

The three of us were alone in what were horrible, appalling circumstances. Yet I wish that I could remember more about that time.

My mother's native language was Gujarati. I only remember a few words in Gujarati, but there are other ways that I connect to my Indian heritage.

I love wearing Indian clothes, and I enjoy cooking Indian food. My favorite Indian food is something that my mother used to make called somossa. It's a small vegetable or chicken dumpling filled with mashed potatoes, and can be spicy or not. I prefer spicy!

❁

My father sent for my mother, my brother and me when I was five years old. I remember little about the actual flight to Costa Rica. I remember being surrounded by darkness and then looking down to the city as we landed. I'd never seen so many lights as these!

Every time I go across the George Washington Bridge in New York, I think of those lights and that night on the plane. It was as though all the stars of heaven were below us and we were headed there. I thought my life was going to be the best.

After we arrived we met up with a friend of my father's. I don't remember her name, but I remember that the first thing we did was to get some ice cream. Mine was green, and lime flavored! I'd never tasted anything like that in my life.

We stayed in the city for two days. Then we finally arrived at our final destination, a small country town called Oriente. That's where we were to be reunited with my father.

I soon learned that the enticing lights below the plane on the night we landed in Costa Rica were *not* the heaven I imagined.

The houses in Costa Rica are often brightly painted, and our wooden house in Oriente was painted pink. There were only about twenty-five or thirty houses; it was one of those places where everybody knows everyone else.

This little town was not rich in any way except its sugar cane and coffee production. The few people who lived in Oriente couldn't keep up with the work in the fields. Migrant workers from Nicaragua would come for the season to fill out the workforce. The workers would only be there for three or four months for the harvest, and then they would move on to the next crop.

To support the family, my father worked as a ranch hand and my mother sold food to the field workers. My brother, Humberto, and I helped her, and it was my job to prepare their drinks. I woke up early, at about 3 o'clock in the morning, to do this. I was so little that I had to climb on a stool to reach what I needed.

Men would come to our house to eat and drink before going to the fields. Later, we would put 50 to 100 lunches in a large wheelbarrow for the workers in the fields. The wheelbarrow was so heavy it made our legs shake as we tried to balance it along the way.

Finally, we would see the men ahead, filling the baskets they had tied around their waists. My brother would sound a large *cacho* (the ox horn he carried) to call the workers in.

*Hooooo! Hoooooooooo!*

Chunches, as we called Humberto, and I loved to pick coffee beans. The beans were so sweet that we ate them right off the stalk. After delivering lunches to the workers, we played like any normal kids, making a game of throwing beans back and forth to each other.

We frequently walked past the Rio Reventazon, exploring along the river's edge on the way home. That river was very beautiful but most people were afraid to swim in it. It was well known that lives had been lost in the strong current. We were afraid of it too, but we sometimes fished there anyway.

Another river, the Rio Pejibaye, was a great part of my childhood. Chunches and I used to go to that river to swim when we were little. We had fun swinging from one bank to the other by grabbing the big branches that overhung the water, like *Tarzan*.

These are some of the more normal memories from my early childhood. There are *other* memories.

# *Fear*

After the migrant workers left for the season, there was a man who stayed behind. My mother introduced him to us as an older brother, and this man stayed and lived with us.

He was my mother's lover.

My father knew it. My father was living in the same house, yet he never said anything about it. Chunches and I soon knew, as well.

One Saturday, like every other Saturday, my father left for the closest city, Turrialba, to buy groceries. My mother took this opportunity to spend time with her lover. That is when she would always send my brother and me to buy cigarettes at the *pulperia*, which is what we called the small local store.

On this particular day, we got to the store before we realized we'd forgotten the money. We had to go back to the house.

The exterior of the house wasn't finished very well. We could easily see inside through the gaps between the wooden planks. That is how we saw them together having sex.

Soon this man, Gilber, started molesting me. I was 5 years old. He came every day to my room and raped me. Every day.

Years passed when I wasn't sleeping like a normal child. I would sit in my bed, dreading the time for him to arrive. Eventually, I didn't even want to fight anymore. I was in shock, I think, and couldn't possibly comprehend what was happening to me.

When I was six or seven years old, I told my mother, "Gilber is touching me and putting something inside me. I'm bleeding."

She pushed me. "You're lying! How could you say something like that? You're a liar!"

I didn't understand why she wouldn't believe me. I decided not to tell her anything else ever again.

Our mother seemed to hate Chunches and me so much. We had no idea why, but she demonstrated this hate regularly.

My mother was always a heavy smoker. She always seemed to have a cigarette in her hand. One of her more frequently used methods of punishment was to put her cigarette out on our arms. If she was the least bit annoyed, and it didn't take much, she would crush her cigarette out on my arm. She wouldn't say anything—what was wrong, or why she was mad. She would just grab my arm and snub out her butt with it. I still have a few faint scars on my arms.

Our mother would beat us until she got too tired to beat us any longer. The beatings got harder and harder, usually lasting until we couldn't even get up. To us, it almost seemed that she was Satan.

She beat us with pretty much anything she could lay her hands on: electrical cords, ropes, whips, sticks, pots. Anything could become an instrument of punishment in her hands. She wouldn't hesitate to punch me with her closed fist. Once, I was doing the dishes after dinner when she announced that she was going out. My back was to her and, under my breath, I mumbled, "You're never here." She heard me. She ran to the sink and punched me in the face so hard that a tooth was knocked right out of my mouth.

Sometimes she would punish us by locking us in a room for the weekend, chained to a table, without food or water. We would do what humans have to do, right there in that little room.

My brother and I helped each other as best we could while we waited in the dark. Long hours would pass until we saw the door knob turn and our mother would enter the room to unchain our feet.

My father was an alcoholic. He was miserable, but he couldn't do anything except for when there was alcohol in his blood. Sometimes he came home drunk and tried to break down the doors. One time he even dared to threaten my mother with a machete. We were behind him pleading, "Papi! Don't do it! You're going to kill her!"

She didn't try to protect us the same way. Just the opposite. She goaded my father, "You gotta hit them! You gotta hit them! You're not mean enough."

Certainly, *she* was mean enough.

One time my father bought a piece of furniture. Back then, furniture was finished with a coating of varnish. I remember that I peeled a little bit of the varnish from that piece of furniture.

My punishment? They pulled all the fingernails from my hand. My father got a hammer. He pounded my fingers until each nail popped out. The pain was so severe that I couldn't do anything for weeks. It was horrible.

Another way they used to torture me was to tie me from my hair, hanging down from the ceiling like a chandelier. Like a *piñata*. And the men who came to our house would go back and forth in that room. But nobody dared to do anything about it because they were so afraid of my mother.

My mother practiced witchcraft. It was known that she would cast spells on people. I saw things that she did that were so powerful. The people in Oriente were so terrified of my mother that no one ever questioned how she treated us, or did anything to try to help my brother and me in any way.

She called me any horrid name she could think of. I was terribly hurt by this and begged her, "Please stop calling me names. Please hit me, I prefer that. Please don't call me names."

They abused me physically. They abused me mentally. This went on for a very long time.

# Fear

The laundry, cooking and cleaning were mostly my responsibility when my mother was out. But just because she wasn't there, didn't mean that she didn't have exacting requirements.

One of the things that I had to do was add *azul* to the white clothes. This bluing is used to take yellow or gray out of white clothes, remove stains and brighten the whites. I washed the clothes by hand in the cement *pila* and hung them out on a clothes line. If my mother saw a stain of any kind, or if the white clothes were not as white as she liked, she would grab me by the hair, and drag me to the clothes line. Then she would make me pull each piece of clothing off the line with my teeth, then wash and hang them again.

He was a year older than me, but I took care of my brother as if I was his mother. I did Chunches' laundry, cooked for him, did everything for him when we were little. He started calling me 'Mami' but I stopped that. "Chunches, I'm not your mother. I'm your sister!"

We cooked over a wood fire. The fire created a layer of black soot on the bottom of the pots, and it was my job to keep these pots shining. First I used a rock to scrape off the soot. Then I used Chumico leaves, with their sandpaper-like finish, to shine the pots. If I missed a spot, or the pots didn't shine to my mother's liking, I could expect a beating. When she finished, she would make me start the whole process all over again.

When we were very young, we were part of a little gang of kids from our school. They all came from broken homes, so we related to them very well. We played outside and did things together.

We all had nicknames for each other. Humberto's nickname, "Chunches," means *trinket*. He got that name because he was always carrying something around, like his machete tied around his waist or some little doodad in his pocket. My nickname was "Garapata," which means *tick,* because I always stuck close to my brother.

Chunches went through a lot and I was there for him. I went through a lot and he was there for me. We were very close, we did everything together.

The way my brother and I would deal with this merciless upbringing was to escape to the rainforest. We would hide for days until my father and mother would either forget whatever made them angry, or would at least calm down.

One time, our mother chased after us with a machete. We were young and some stupid thing we did set her off. When we saw how mad she was, and saw the machete she had in her hand, we ran away as fast as we could.

It made her even more angry that she couldn't catch up. So she threw the machete directly at us! It caught Chunches on the lower side of his leg, about at his ankle. To this day, I can still see it vibrating there. He pulled it out and we ran for the relative safety of the woods.

I remembered some old women talking about spider webs being used to treat injuries. So when we were in the trees away from the house, we looked for a spider web, I pulled it out of the tree and put it in the cut! We were just two little kids, trying to survive. He still has that scar.

During those times when we hid in the woods, we would sleep up in a tree, making sure to find the best branch so that we wouldn't fall down. There were dangerous animals in the rainforest in Costa Rica. One time a wolf tried to climb the tree we were in. We were screaming as we watched him clawing at the tree trunk, knowing he wanted to eat us.

We would catch and eat whatever we could find in the forest. I have eaten things that people would never eat or even imagine eating. It was the survival instinct. Chunches fished, and we would even eat insects. Also raccoons, snakes, armadillo, worms, and pretty much anything that we could catch.

One time when we were swimming, there was an alligator in the lake. We always carried *machetes* with us and Chunches used his knife to fight and kill the alligator. We ate off of him for days.

We did what we had to in order to survive. We would run in the rainforest and live in the elements out in the open woods.

One day we didn't realize that our mother's lover, Gilber, was following us and found where we were hiding in the woods. He caught my brother and he raped him.

There was nothing I could do to rescue my brother. I hid behind a huge Ceiba tree. I knew Chunches was getting raped. I heard his screaming.

I had such a hard time to forgive myself because I didn't do anything to help my brother. But I was very young. And it happened to me too. After he raped my brother, he raped me.

When Chunches and I were a little older, we moved to a different house. This house was also made of wood, this time painted blue.

The house was divided into three sections. The first section had the living room and bedrooms, all with hardwood floors. From there, you would step down into the dining room which had cement floors. Attached to that was the kitchen, which had dirt floors, and led outside to another cement floor and the pila for laundry. The cement and dirt floors would need frequent sweeping, just like in the pink house.

The hardwood floors brought new chores. It was my job to keep the hardwood floors not only clean but also waxed until they shone. First I had to scrub them on my hands and knees. Then I had to use a paste wax to shine them. After the floors were waxed, I buffed them to a high gloss using rags under to my feet.

My mother would come in when I finished, stand in the light and look for her reflection on the floor. If they weren't mirror-shined and she didn't see her reflection, she would drag her feet all over, until the entire floor was scuffed. Then I would have to do it all over again. My hands would hurt, and my knees and back would ache after that.

In front of the blue house was a large water apple tree, what we call *manzana de agua*. We had a German Shepherd, and I would tie the dog to this tree.

One day when we arrived home, we found a huge snake around the dog's neck. It had killed our dog. We killed the snake and then we ate it. It felt good to have revenge for our dog.

The blue house faced a decrepit rooming house. When I opened the window in my room, I would face this large brown shack. This beat-up building looked like it could fall down at any time. This is where the migrant workers would stay when they worked the coffee fields.

When I opened the window, there was nothing but men. It was disgusting. I saw them through that window, doing things that I should never have seen.

# *Rejection*

At the age of nine my mother said to me, "Sioni, I want to take you to the city. We're going to take the train."

I was so happy because I was finally going to do something with my mother. For a young girl, a train ride with my mother was going to be quite an adventure.

The moment we boarded the train I asked, "Mami, can I sit by the window?"

She looked at me, no smile, no hint of what would come. Just, "Okay." Nothing else.

I watched as other people got on and stored their bags in overhead bins. I wondered if they were going to the city too, and what they would do there.

The train stopped in the little towns along the way. It was exciting to look out that window to see all those towns and people! I was convinced that I was quite special because I was going all the way to the city.

I didn't know that I was about to be introduced into the underworld of human trafficking.

I remember arriving at the house. There were a lot of different rooms. In the middle, there was an atrium, a kind of inner garden. There were women there. Right next door to the house there was a bar.

The lady who ran the house, Lila, was about five feet tall and a bit overweight. She was light-skinned and she used a lot of makeup. Her eyebrows were penciled in a very dark brown, which to me made her look quite scary. She wore high heels, had gold teeth, and curly hair.

Lila worked at the bar as a bartender. The bar was right next door, and it was easy for customers to go from one establishment to the other. If you stepped out of the house, there was a sidewalk, and that's where the main street was. As you walked out into the sidewalk, you could make a quick turn right into the bar next to the house.

The big, old house had paint that was starting to chip away, and both it and the bar were quite shabby. In Costa Rica, which is very close to the equator, it always feels like summer. Because of this, the bar kept the doors open to let the air circulate. They had a large juke box, what we called a *rocola*, with a lot of lights on it. It was so loud that you could easily hear it outside with the doors open. There was always music from the 50's and 60's playing. The older guys would end up crying because they were so sentimental about the music when they were drunk.

It never entered my mind that my own mother was going to leave me in the hands of evil. But she left me there. Lila said to me, "Your *mamita* wants you to stay in this room. I'm going to bring you some food. Don't cry. Your mother will be back for you later."

At first, even though I was a little afraid, I was excited. I was a little girl from the country and I was amazed by all the sights and sounds of the city. I wondered when my mother would come back I thought she might take me to see more of the city.

In my little girl's mind, I thought that Lila had gone to get some toys for me to play with, so I wouldn't miss my mother. I remember waiting with eagerness, to see what dolls she would bring me.

Of course she was lying to me when she told me my mother would be back for me. But I didn't know it at the time. "You need to stop crying, this man is going to come to see you," Lila told me. "He is a shoemaker, so if you are good to him he will give you a new pair of shoes. Do whatever he asks you to do." He was a grown man, and I was only nine years old. I remember being nervous and afraid.

I was in a little room that faced the interior patio. I don't think there was anybody there that day except Lila. She was back and forth to the bar where she was working. I realize now that she was checking on me, making sure that I didn't leave.

The shoemaker had not arrived yet. It was around 5 or 6 o'clock because the sun was going down. I noticed that Lila had left the door to the house slightly open when she walked out, and I was able to sneak outside. She didn't see me sitting on the one little step on the sidewalk. I started crying again. And then I decided to cross the street.

I made it to the other side where there was a gas station. I'll never forget the *Gasolinera La Castellana.* In fact, it's still there. I was by the phone booth when a man came over to me. He said, "Little girl. Why are you crying?"

"I want to go home! I want to go home!"

I told him I lived in Oriente. I didn't know much about it and I didn't know how to describe how to get there. Luckily, even though it was a pretty small town, he knew where it was.

The man took me in his car and he drove me the two and a half hours back to my town. When I got to our house, I was so happy to be back home and to see my mother. I remember the first thing she said. "Why are you here? Why did you come back?"

I saw her face and she had a look of both surprise and disgust. At that moment, I realized that she did not want me. Maybe she never did.

She rejected me. but I had to stay there. There was no place else for me to go. That man, Gilber, was still living there. The sexual abuse continued.

Now that I look back, I may have been a threat to my mother while this man, Gilber, was abusing me. It could be that my mother thought she had to get rid of me because something could come of it. I don't know, but she wanted to be rid of me. She wanted to get me out of her life. It got to the point that my very presence would bother her.

But I didn't have any other place to belong.

It wasn't only that she wanted the money she got for selling me to Lila. Perhaps it wasn't about the money at all.

Sometimes I get very emotional. Even though we don't get to choose who our parents are going to be, I sure wish I could have had good parents. But I'm a grown adult now; I don't need them anymore. I'vecome to realize that I never had real parents anyway. They were never there for me.

There's one thing about my family, they always kept things to themselves. They didn't talk much about their lives or what they did or how things came to be. The day we met him was the first time we'd ever heard of Walter.

"Okay. This is your brother. Say 'hello' to your brother."

Walter is a half-brother. He was my mother's son, but quite a bit older than Chunches and I. He didn't come with us when we moved from India. He was already in Costa Rica.

Walter was abused by my parents, as Chunches and I were. Because of this, he would leave for long periods of time. I never had a close connection with him like a brother because he was never much a part of my life that way. He never really felt like a brother.

Eventually, he went away to trade school to learn to repair radios. He always had a lot of girlfriends with him. But there was a time when he stayed home longer.

And that's when he started abusing me. I had just run away from Lila. Now I was getting abused from both Gilber *and* my older brother.

I could go on and on with this for hours telling you all the things they did to me. But what good would that do?

## *Hopeless*

In Costa Rica, people live in very open houses. Because of the hot weather, the first thing we did in the morning is open the windows and doors to catch the breeze. There wasn't glass in the windows like most of the other houses in our country town. Instead, there was a big piece of wood inserted into the window frame if you wanted to "close the window."

In the blue house, you could walk into the living room, down a step, then straight through the kitchen and dining room. This led out to a huge open room where we did our laundry. With the doors open, I could hear the animals: roosters, chickens, birds, and squirrels; all the sounds of the country.

And with the doors open, everyone from the neighborhood could see us when we were doing laundry in the huge pila.

The outside laundry area had three big metal walls. The one wall that faced to the neighbor's house was open. You could see from the inside (looking out), but not as well from the outside (looking in).

Men would come to the house to look for my mother. If she wasn't there, they would feel free to rape me. I don't know if my mother knew how they abused me. I believe she knew they would come when I was going to be by myself.

I never asked her if she knew what they were doing to me. Considering the other things that happened, I wonder if these men were paying her for me.

I fought back with one of them once and told him to leave me alone, but I gave up when it didn't do any good.

There was a neighbor woman, who lived very close to us. One time she heard me screaming, and later, when my mother was there, she asked if I was okay.

My mother explained it away. "Yes, she's okay. She's fine. You know she's just a screamer." I couldn't find a way to speak up for myself.

Some of the men who came were maintenance men from the school where my mother was a teacher. Often these men were with her drinking at the bars, so they would come looking for her. If my mother was not home, which was most of the time, and I was home alone, they wouldn't wait for her. Instead, they would take the opportunity to abuse me.

After a while, I got used to the abuse and I didn't fight anymore. I used to think it was better not to fight and not get killed. Not that I knew for sure that they were going to kill me. But that's what I used to think.

By that time it didn't hurt me anymore. The first time when I was only five it hurt terribly, and I bled so much. But after awhile I figured out what to expect.

One time, after he was done, one of the men said, "You know, you are not your mother's daughter." That hurt me so much. It hurt me more than what he did to me.

"You are *huérfano*." This is the Spanish word for 'orphan' and he taunted me with this to me several times. I cried and called him a liar, but he insisted it was true. "Go ask your mother," he said.

It hurt me a lot to hear what he said, so I asked her. She said, "Shut up you stupid! Why are you saying that?"

"Because Reinaldo told me so."

"Aw, don't listen to that stupid man."

So I don't know if what he told me is true. I never questioned her again. But if she brought me from India, then I must be her child. I remember the flight from India, so I must be hers.

I recall crying a lot about the thought of being an orphan, but not so much about the physical abuse. I don't remember thinking about anything when they were raping me.

I couldn't find a way to make the abuse stop. I don't remember my exact age, but I was living in the blue house. I was so tired of getting raped by Gilber every day, that I decided to kill myself before I would let it happen again, even one more time.

*I'm not going to allow this! I'm just going to die tonight if I have to.*

I brought a knife to my room that night.

We had no bathroom in this house. If it was dark, I was afraid to go outside to use the latrine. Instead, I would pee through the floorboards in my room. Anything so that I wouldn't have to walk out there.

On this night there was moonlight—the moon was so big that you could actually see the shadow of people. And I was so afraid of those people.

Before long, Gilber came and pushed open the wooden window and jumped into my bedroom. I could see his shadow and I knew it was him. When he jumped into my room, he landed in my pee. I was ready. I had already decided what to do.

I got my knife. I was going to kill him—or myself—rather than go through that again.

As he came after me, I grabbed the knife. I could see the knife in my hand through the shadows. I started kicking the door of my bedroom, yelling for my father. "Papi! Papi! There's someone in my room!" I was so determined that this man would not touch me. I didn't care if I had to die that night in the process.

I heard my mother from the other room, telling my father, "Oh that stupid girl... there she goes again. She's paranoid!"

But my father came and tried to turn the light on. Nothing happened. The electricity to the house was powered by a switch on the outside wall. Gilber had turned off the lights in the house before he came in.

Chunches was there and he stood up for me. He had been hurt in this house too. My mother called me a liar.

Chunches was so angry that he yelled at her. "You go and leave us here. My daddy will take care of us. My sister will cook. Leave—go with him!"

Gilber left the house that night. In the morning, because he had stepped in my pee, Gilber's footprints were in my room. They could clearly be seen leading from the window to my bed. I thought, *Now! Now they will believe me, and protect me!*

But that didn't happen. They never protected me.

Unfortunately, that would not be the last we saw of him. Gilber left for a while, but our mother stayed. He moved to the next town. Mother would go to visit him, and soon he came back.

I skipped school on many days, but at least I did go to school. One week I would attend in the morning and the next I would be there in the afternoon.

The school was very small. The yard had a flagpole, and was enclosed by chain link fencing. This fencing was surrounded by Naranja trees. At recess, we would go out and climb those trees to pick the oranges to eat.

A little sidewalk led into the pink cinderblock school. An elementary school in Costa Rica consists of grades 1—6, and these grades were combined into the four classrooms. The four metal doors lined the long hallway, each one painted a different color: blue, red, pink, and yellow.

The front classroom was the largest, and the teacher's desk was the first thing you came to when you entered the room. This teacher's name was Tañada, and I remember her as being very mean to us.

I was not a pleasant student. I was very angry, and would let my frustrations out on the teacher. My little gang of friends and I would give this teacher a very hard time. We made her life miserable, so she would smack us our hands with her ruler. She had another punishment, which was to go to the corner, where we were to be on our knees on hard-baked corn. We might be there for 20 minutes, with the kernels digging into our knees, before we were allowed to stand up.

I remember going to the school with cuts and bruises all over my body, especially on my legs. Our mother still beat us regularly, using anything at hand to hurt us with. I didn't like to wear dresses because the scars on my legs would be clearly visible, and for many years I felt ashamed.

I washed the uniforms that Chunches and I wore, but still I often felt dirty. I wondered why I couldn't have a nice mother. Other kids had good mothers.

There were two girls in particular, Cathy and Janet. I really disliked these two girls. It wasn't their fault. Their only offense was that they had good mothers when I did not. Their hair was always brushed and their uniforms were always ironed. They had the nicest book bags. I hated them because of it, and would get in fights with them, pulling their hair and such. I was hurt because they had mothers who took care of them, and I didn't.

There was one time that was special, though. When I was about eight or nine years old, my mother took the day off. Now, my mother was an alcoholic who drank every single day. She would even go to school with a bottle of wine in her pocketbook. But she never missed a day from work. Ever.

Except for this one day, this one glorious day. And on this day she stayed home from work. She helped me to get ready for school! She brushed my hair, and put it in two braids. On that day, I felt like the most beautiful and special girl in the world. The other girls noticed right away and told me how lovely I looked. I told them it was my mother who brushed my hair. To me that was so precious.

My mother was one of the two women who taught in my school. I don't really know how she got the job as a teacher. Maybe it was because she was friends with the other teacher.

It could be because she was sleeping with the school's director. One day I went to the school to find her, but I didn't see her anywhere. I checked the pantry where they kept the supplies, and I found her. She was on the floor, having sex with the director of the school.

We were not able to be consistent with our attendance at school, especially when we stayed in the mountains. Still, Chunches and I went through the grades. He was left back one year, but I never was. Even with all the absences, we graduated from elementary school together in 1982. It was likely because of our mother's affair with the school's director, but we got our certificates.

# *Trust*

*A*buela (Gramma) Lili lived right in the middle of the rainforest. She wasn't a blood relative, but I wish she had been. Sometimes after school on the weekends, I would go to see her. It took over two hours to walk to her, crossing the mountains, but I loved to visit with her.

When I got close to her house I would whistle to let her know it was me. She would be waiting for me at the door, waving her hands. Her warm welcome was extremely special to me.

The sky would start getting dark around 5 o'clock. It became completely dark in her home in the forest because her wooden house had no electricity. When I read the story about Hansel and Gretel, I always thought this was what it was like to be there. Except without her trying to eat me!

Beyond the effort it took to cross the mountains, there was another danger getting to her house. There was a guy in one of the houses on the way who would watch for me. His house was about 30 minutes from Abuela's house. He knew I was coming because he could see me approach on the path.

One day, he offered me a few trinkets in exchange for me to let him touch me. He threw me on the floor, and got on top of me. He kissed my neck, and touched me, all over my body, his hand ending up between my legs. He didn't rape me, but the molestation did enough damage.

When I told Abuela about it, she was so angry! She wanted to protect me. She went to look for him at his house. Abuela told his mother what he had done to me. Of course, the mother denied the whole thing, calling me a big liar. And the next time he got me in the mountains, he badgered me, asking why

I was lying about him. But he left me alone after that.

More than anything, I appreciated how Abuela protected me. Why were people always hurting me? Everywhere I went, it seemed, people were out to get me. I wonder if a lot of kids went through what I did. There were a lot of perverts in that town.

The first thing Abuela would do when I arrived was to cook a meal for me. She had a large cement stove where she would build a fire to cook on. She used to hang meat over the stove to dry, to make what we would call jerky.

I loved being there with her. We would talk, and I knew that she cared for me a lot.

I would sleep with her because I was afraid of the wolves that would come to her porch. Sometimes you could hear them calling each other by howling from Abuela's porch. The louder they would get, the closer I would get to her!

She would say, "Don't be scared, they're not going to hurt you. They've been doing that for years!" We could hear the wolves sleeping on her porch. Having so many wolves right outside the door was pretty intense—but then I liked the adventure of it.

Early in the morning, around dawn, they would start leaving her porch. There were holes in the wooden planks that made up her house, and I could peek through to see the outside. I could see that they were incredibly beautiful animals. They were huge, with big eyes and fur of different colors. They were magnificent animals! They were vicious, though. Sometimes you could hear them fighting in the night, which was pretty scary.

When I was there with Abuela, I could sleep. Nobody was going to touch me, no one was going to do anything to me. I was able to have a peaceful sleep because of my Abuela's protection.

Because she didn't have running water in her cabin, we had to go to the river to bathe. And because I loved Abuela so much, I would wash her clothes in the river. And I had fun swimming at the same time.

I made a rig to help me haul water. I hung full buckets on either end of a branch that I balanced on my shoulders to make the load easier to carry. I would bring 20–25 buckets of water to her house so that she wouldn't have to do it by herself.

In the evenings we would go to a part of her *finca* (farm) to watch the sun go down. It was the most beautiful scene. The red sky was bright and the sun was like a giant sunflower. As the sun set and it got dark, we would hurry to get home. She'd say, "We need to cross the mountain before it gets dark and the wolves come back!"

It was exciting to me—both beautiful and mysterious. We went to that same spot every time I was there. There was peace in that place.

Sometimes she and I would take a walk to find fruit from the forest to eat. Sometimes we would go to town for provisions that she needed. It was a long walk from her place to the town, so if we needed to go there we would ride her horses, and pack her purchases on the back of one of them for the trip home.

I cared for this woman as if she was my actual grandmother. I first met her one Easter when my father and I went to pick up palm branches from her. She supported herself by living off the land. She owned a large property, and she rented a few parcels of it for income. She also had coffee beans, and I used to help her to collect the beans to sell.

There weren't any other kids who went up there when I did, but this lady had raised 12 children who did not belong to her. They belonged to her husband who had passed away. She never bore a child of her own.

Of those 12 children, the youngest daughter was in her 40's. When my father met this daughter, he had an affair with her. I learned this because my father would take me to the pueblo on Saturdays, ostensibly to buy groceries.

I would try to look nice on these excursions. I made my rubber shoes shiny by polishing them with butter until they looked like patent leather. I would walk very carefully to make sure they didn't get scuffed. But the dogs would smell the butter and they wanted to lick my shoes!

"Tsch! Tsch! Get out of here, dog! *Bayase!*"

At that time, my father was drinking heavily and would go to the bar, leaving me outside. I used to buy candy, and eat it outside while I was waiting for him. I must have dozed off one day while I was waiting. It was only for a short time, but when I woke up, one of my shoes wasn't shiny anymore! I needed to stay awake if I was going to protect my shoe shine from the dogs!

My father would take me because if he didn't it would be very suspicious to my mother. But this made me the 'third wheel.'

In the bar, I could see a woman who I knew to be Abuela's daughter. She and my father sat at the bar together, having a good time.

One time I asked my father to do something for me that he didn't want to do. I didn't think before I spoke, but I said very loudly, "You know, Papi. I saw you with that lady with her head on your shoulder." I said this in front of my mother. She got so mad that I thought she would kill my father.

I was miserable because I had done something horrible to get my father into trouble. My mother kicked my father out. He started sleeping outside on a pile of wood, but he never left the property.

I felt so guilty that I would go outside at night and give him a pillow and blanket, and I brought food to him. But he never left. My mother believed that he was cheating with this woman, and she didn't want him back. It was a very hard situation.

One day, my Abuela Lili was getting on the bus that I was on with my mother. The bus had stopped, and people were getting on and off.

My mother and I were coming off, and Abuela Lili was coming on. When my mother saw her, she kicked her so hard in the chest, that 80-year-old Abuela Lili fell down and broke her hip.

I felt horrible, but I felt caught between two worlds. I couldn't go and rescue Abuela Lili. I was there with my mother, who knew my father was fooling around with her daughter. But then again, Abuela treated me better than my own mother. I didn't know what to do, so I started crying.

I didn't know if I was crying for what my mother did to Abuela or because my Abuela was on the floor and I couldn't help her. That guilt was with me for a long time.

Anything having to do with me visiting Abuela Lili stopped immediately. My mother didn't allow me to talk to her or to visit with her. Abuela Lili became an enemy to my mother. Even though this lady was very special to me, our relationship was broken.

*I didn't see her again for 3 or 4 years until after my daughter was born. I was in the city and alone with my baby daughter when I saw her. I ran to her and was relieved and grateful to find out that she held nothing against me.*

*It was especially important to me that she was able to hold Scheila, who was only a couple months old. It was beautiful. We went out to the market and we had coffee and talked.*

*Shortly after that chance meeting, she died. Seeing her again had been very special. My relationship with Abuela Lili was another thing that my mother had taken away from me, but I got to see Abuela one more time.*

# *Faith*

The little pulperia was an old fashioned store. We would walk up to the wooden counter and give our order to the shopkeeper, Don Emiliano. Oriente was in the middle of nowhere, so they had no fresh vegetables or meat at this store. They carried cigarettes, and this is where my mother would send my brother and me when she needed a new pack.

My mother was a very hard person. She wouldn't simply tell us to go to the store to get her a new pack. Instead, she would spit on the floor. She would warn us to be fast about it. "If this spit is dry before you come back, I'm going to beat you guys up."

We would go through the woods running—always barefoot, but as fast as we could go—so we could get home in time.

One time my mother told me to go get some rice and beans from the pulperia. It was pretty far from our home, about an hour and a half trip if we went through the woods.

I got to the store to pick up the food, but I heard a jangling sound I had never heard before. It was coming from the house across the street. I walked into the house and found that it was a family that was having a church service in their home. The sound I heard was the tambourine they used to keep time with the songs they were singing.

As a 12-year-old, I was very curious about what was going on. I walked straight into the house to find out. They didn't know me, but when I walked in they made me feel so good—*so loved*—that I stayed.

*Whether it's at church or at home, at a meeting or a social function, to welcome people warmly is one of the most important things that we can do. I learned this from my experience with these people.*

*Whenever I am at a church or at an event, I remember what it felt like to be a stranger who was given a sincere and open welcome. When I see a new face, I introduce myself, offer them a friendly greeting and welcome them in this same way.*

*The kindness shown to me by that family made a lasting impact on my life. I hope that in some small way, I can do the same for someone else whenever the opportunity presents itself.*

After that, I would visit the house as often as I could. It was far, but still walking distance from my house. I would go on Tuesdays and Sundays, and I definitely looked forward to being there. I felt the warmth and the love, the passion and the peace with these people.

Tuesday's meetings were at nighttime. We were there from 6 to 7:30. After that, we all sat together and had a little portion of bread and some coffee. It was very humble, and a very small group. In fact, everyone there was related to each other.

On Sundays, we had a service at 9 in the morning and it ended at 10:30 or 11 AM More often than not, the service would run long. They were fully devoted to their faith, and not in a hurry to finish.

I was very young, so I don't remember everything they taught me. I didn't grasp a lot of it because it was all new to me. I know that it was about the New Testament and love. Most importantly, I felt the love of these people.

I do remember very clearly one thing that I was taught. My pastor would teach from 1 John, "How are you going to say you love God, even if you have not seen Him? But you're going to hate someone who's right in front of you where you can see and touch him? If we say we have God in us, we have love, because God is full of love."

*I use this now when I teach in the women's prison. I tell them, 'I know that you're here with people who have different habits and different issues. It can be difficult to get along. But how are you going to say that you love God if you don't like your cellmate? You say you love God, but you can't see God, can't touch God. And you can actually have an encounter with your cellmate; you can talk to her.' I always make that connection. I remember him talking a lot about that, and it's stuck with me for many years.*

**Whoever claims to love God yet hates a brother or sister is a liar. For whoever does not love their brother and sister, whom they have seen, cannot love God, whom they have not seen.**

**1 John 4:20**

# Rejoice

I got baptized in the Rio Pacuare when I was 12 years old. None of my relatives were there, but my church family was all there. It was a great experience.

Everyone brought sandwiches and sodas. When you're little, you like to eat. Anytime there was going to be food, I was going to be there! I didn't eat a lot of good food when I was growing up. It was a treat for me when they cooked and shared with me.

We would go to a different home each Sunday. The home that hosted the meeting would make a big pot of soup with lots of ingredients, including meat. How I eagerly anticipated that Sunday meal!

Early on, I invited my father to go to church with me. He came and would walk with me. It was *so* good! We would sing as we went along, and it was so nice to be crossing the mountains and singing with him. Sometimes I would howl, just to hear the echo! That was pretty cool.

We were invited to meetings in different homes during the week. We had to walk some distance through the rainforest to get there. The meetings started late in the evening on Tuesdays. We would start walking at 5 or 5:30 in the afternoon, depending on the distance. By that time in the evening, the decreasing light in the rainforest casts dark shadows. We would bring our flashlights to light the way. I walked very close to the others because I was afraid to be far from the safety of the group.

We could hear the mountain lions, the wolves, and the owls along with the other birds. And the monkeys! Costa Rica has huge monkeys and that was pretty scary for a little kid. My father didn't have a good singing voice—neither of us did. But we used to sing to block out the sound of the animals and the night noises. All in all, it was a fun adventure.

There was one night we got invited to a home that had no lights. We read the Bible and had our service by candlelight. We shared coffee and bread before we left at 8:30 or 9 PM. We had to cross through the woods, and over the mountains again to get home.

My daddy and the other older people said spooky things to try to frighten the other little kids and me.

"Papi! Papi! Help me! There's something coming behind us!" We were scared, but we knew their teasing was all in fun!

My father had an *acordeón* (accordion). He had learned how to play it when he was a young boy. When he realized that the only instruments at our little services were one guitar and one tambourine, he decided to bring his accordion. The accordion made a lot of noise, but it was good to have some more music to accompany the singing.

Chunches never went to service with us. He wasn't at all interested. When I would invite him, he would say, "No, I don't want to go there. That's not for me."

My father stopped going to church because my mother made him feel guilty. "You're going again? You're leaving me alone when I'm not feeling good?"

Every time that we were ready to leave, the devil would be working behind the scenes. When we were ready to go, there was always a problem. My mother was very unhappy that my father would leave home to go to meeting with me. In the meantime, she would go to the bars and come in late. But she would want my daddy in the house, even though she wasn't even there. She used to get very angry. Over time, Papi stopped going to church with me to avoid having confrontations with her.

My mother would tell fortunes by reading Tarot cards and 'throwing the shells'. As far as I know, she never used witchcraft try to stop us from going to church. She never said anything to me. But she told my father, "You'd better stop going to that church. If you don't, I'm going to do something to you, and afterward you won't be able to get out of the bed!"

So my father was feeling guilty and very afraid. He loved God and going to church, but he believed her threats. And he believed that she was capable of doing what she said she would do.

When my father stopped coming to church, the pastor asked about where he was. They were a loving congregation, and they were concerned about him.

I was young and didn't know better, so I told him exactly what happened. "My mother is very mad. She says if he continues to come to church she'd going to do something to him and he's not going to be able to walk again."

The pastor was shocked. "In the name of Jesus, I rebuke that!" He never asked me again!

Everybody in our small town was intimidated by her. Once it got around that her spells had worked, then everyone believed that her witchcraft was real and powerful.

My mother didn't approve of my going to church, but she didn't stop me so I continued to attend. That's how I came to know Christ at this young age.

They were very friendly and nice. They never talked about my mother. They never questioned me about her and I appreciated that. She was infamous in this town and certainly, everyone knew about her. But they never made me feel like an outsider.

When I came home from church, I knew I was still going to be abused that night. And I knew it was wrong.

Then, a few months later, I had to stop going to this church. My mother had other plans for me.

## Protected By God

I had my first period when I was 12 years old. And I had a couple miscarriages from when I was very young. The reality is, I got pregnant a couple times, and my mother forced my abortions.

The first time that I missed my period, I was still less than 13 years old. My mother noticed that I was getting sick in the mornings. She looked me over closely.

"You're pregnant."

I had no idea if it was true.

She took me to *el dispensario* where the doctor would come once a week, and they provided some basic care. Things like sprains and checking for high blood pressure. That's where we found out for sure that I was pregnant.

When we got home, my mother made a concoction using the seed of an avocado mashed with aspirin and birth control pills. It was a disgusting potion. She made me drink it and soon after I got my period. I remember the pieces of something like blood coming out. I had miscarried.

I knew what the drink was supposed to do. At first, I wanted to keep the baby, but I knew that my mother would never allow it. I had mixed feelings. I was afraid, and I was embarrassed. I wondered what people would say or think about me. Still, I thought it would have been nice to have a baby— someone to love, and someone who would love me back.

She subjected me to be used by men, and got extremely angry with me when I got pregnant but never showed me how to avoid it. Of course, to her, getting pregnant was my own fault!

When I was 13 years old, my mother said to me, "I want to take you to the city because I want you to be a baby sitter."

There was some sadness because I was leaving my brother. But he was already starting his life working in the fields. Other than that, I was happy when she told me this. I thought that I was finally going to get away from the abuse, the anger, the beatings, and from her. In fact, I was eager to go.

In my young girl's mind, I imagined working for a nice, kind family in a cozy, little house. I pictured myself taking care of a baby, smiling, feeling peaceful and safe.

But of course, that was not her plan.

She *did* leave me at a house.

We stepped off of the bus in San Pedro and walked across the street. It was starting to get dark. I recall feeling anxious, but I was still holding on to the idea of being the nanny for a good family.

When we got to the house my mother pressed a button and the door slid to the side. We went down two steps into a small dark alley that opened right into the kitchen of the house. We walked up a flight of stairs and entered a large, dimly lit, miserable room. There were three old metal beds, each with a little night stand, and separated by dingy curtains that hung from the ceiling.

Two girls, only a little older than me, were there. They each sat on a bed and it was clear that they were waiting for me. Later I learned their names—Maritza and Margarita. As they approached me, I turned to see Mami quickly going down the stairs.

She never said goodbye, and she never looked back. She just left me there. Again, she had sold me like chattel.

"Human trafficking" wasn't a term we used back then. All I knew was that I was now a captive of people who didn't think of me as a person at all. I was a slave.

The two girls tried to comfort me after my mother left, but they weren't able to explain to me the deal my mother had made.

There were two guys who lived there too. They were the 'dogs.' Their job was to make sure that we were okay. They came and explained to me exactly what I was there for.

I stayed there for three years, forced to have sex with men—sometimes five or six men in a day. On weekends there were more customers. They gave us birth control pills to make sure we didn't get pregnant. The only break from this was when I got my period.

The two guys were supposed to be there for our protection. But they were just using us too. Anytime they wanted, they would come and get us. It seemed that I was more subject to go through this than the older ones. They seemed to like having a new, younger girl.

The other two girls would get drunk or high because they didn't want to deal with the reality of our wretched lives. I never drank and I never did drugs. I found my refuge in what I had learned about Jesus, who I knew was my Savior.

I had the experience of learning about Jesus when I was 12 years old. It helped me to know that God was going to take me out of that place one day. I didn't know when or how, but I knew that He was not going to allow me to go through that life forever.

So when men used me, I would block my pain by thinking about flowers and gardens. Instead of turning to drugs, I would think, *God is going to take me out of here.*

I told Maritza and Margarita that God would rescue them too, if they accepted him. They would ridicule me. "How can you talk about God this way? How?"

"God's going to take *me* out of this place."

They would snap back, almost angrily, "How can you believe that? Look where you are! Look what's happening to you!"

But I knew with certainty, because of the experience that I had in that house across from the pulperia. The devout Christians living there had taught me about God's promises to those who believe in Him. When

I accepted Jesus as my Lord and Savior, I had proclaimed my trust in Him. My belief remained absolute.

When I was deep in pain and being used, I would repeat the words the pastor said in that church.

"No matter what you are going through in life, God will never leave or forsake you. Even when you don't see Him, He is watching you. He loves you."

*Even today, when trouble comes, I reach back and find comfort in those precious words. I believe them because God was my Protector, even back in that sad place. He kept me from spiraling down as the other girls did. He watched over me. No one else did. If not for God, how could I have survived?*

*...because God has said, "Never will I leave you; never will I forsake you."*
*So we say with confidence, "The Lord is my helper; I will not be afraid.*
*What can mere mortals do to me?"*

*Hebrews 13:4-6*

I was captive there for about three years. Those years made me be strong. And I learned to hate men, I hated them with my whole being. I wanted to escape, but there didn't seem to be a way.

They didn't waste much money taking care of us. The conditions we lived in were deplorable. Feeding us was not much of a priority. Ramen noodles were a staple item for us. We kept a hot plate in our second floor bathroom to cook the soup.

One day, we forgot to put water in the pot that was heating up on the hot plate. The smell of the burning noodles filled the house, and the dogs came to see what was going on. The windows were always kept locked. But for this they unlocked and opened the tiny bathroom window to let air circulate. They went downstairs to get some water to put the fire out.

That's when I realized that even though the other girls could not, I was small enough to fit through that window! I jumped from the second story, and fell into a huge bush. It hurt, but I didn't think about the pain then. I ran until I got to the school where I knew from years earlier that there was a bus stop. I crossed the street, and came to the wide avenue with buses going up and down the street, picking up passengers.

I was old enough to be able to take the bus back to Oriente alone, but I didn't have any money. When I jumped, I didn't take anything with me.

I got on the bus and waited nervously for the *conductor*, the bus driver who would come to collect my fare. I knew that they would stop the bus right where it was, and kick me off because I didn't have the fare. I'd seen it before. They didn't care about anyone's excuses.

The man came, and I began to beg him not to put me out. The woman who sat next to me could sense that I was truly in trouble, and she generously paid my bus fare!

God had put this kind woman on my path for this purpose, I'm sure of it!

This may have seemed a small incident to her, but to me it was an extraordinary act of kindness. I was relieved and grateful to be safely on my way back to Oriente. I made my escape. I was long gone before anyone in the house knew what happened.

I got back to my mother, again.

Again.

There wasn't any other place for me to go. That was the place I called home.

# Mistakes

When my older brother, Walter, was 17 or 18 years old, he started dating a woman. One night he went to visit her and came back home around midnight, bringing her with him. In the early '80s in Costa Rica, if you brought a woman home, you stayed with her. After a time, she got pregnant and had a daughter. They got married.

There was a family celebration, but I was still under lock and key in the city and didn't know anything about it at the time. I remember seeing pictures of her in her wedding dress, and they did get married in a church. Thankfully, after he got married, Walter left me alone.

My mother found fault in everyone, and her new daughter-in-law was no exception. She didn't like her because she was very young. She was 16 or 17 years old, and she didn't know how to do the chores to take care of the house. To my mother, this was reason enough for her incessant talk about how her daughter-in-law was not a good wife.

Gilber had gone to another town, but he came back to the blue house after about a month. When I escaped after being sold for the second time, I clearly recall him still sneaking around.

He was only there a short time longer, though. There were charges on him by my sister-in-law, Walter's wife. She found him raping my little niece, who was only 3 or 4 years old. We found out that he also abused a cousin of ours. He had to flee the area because the police were now after him.

I remember one time when I was in my room crying. I felt like no one did anything for me when Gilber was doing these things to me. But when my sister-in-law caught him doing this to my niece, she went right to the authorities, and they went after him. I felt betrayed. They did everything in their power to protect my niece and to stop Gilber. Why didn't anybody do that for me?

I have no idea what happened to Gilber. Years went by and my sister-in-law said he had some contact with my mother, but that was all.

On another occasion, when I got pregnant again, my mother took me by bus to the city, to a lady who did abortions. They used a wire hanger to do the job. I got very ill. I thought I would die because I lost such a large amount of blood. She must have ripped something inside me. I remember how it pinched my insides when I tried to sit afterward. It was awful.

I had the abortion in the morning, and in the afternoon we got back on the bus. Exhausted and still feeling a lot of pain in my abdomen, I looked blindly out the bus window. I thought I must be the worst person in the world

I still a young teenager, but I understood what I had just done. I felt worthless. Everything that happened to me caused nothing but pain. I wondered if anything good would ever happen to me.

I was looking out the window and crying, but my mother said, "Aw, get over it. It's no big deal."

That coolness from her—she didn't show me an ounce of compassion. She never said, "I'm so sorry." Instead, it was, "Shake it off and get over it."

I felt guilty because I believed that I had done something wrong in God's eyes. I knew what was right and what was wrong. But I felt like I had no other choice but to do what my mother told me to do. I didn't have the power to do anything else.

I was staring at my mother when she fell asleep on the bus and I hated her so much for being so heartless. I wondered, *Why couldn't I have a mother who cared for me and would treat me right? Why was it that she couldn't even do one nice thing for me?*

I wondered why I could never get a break. *When will I ever get to laugh and smile and be myself without having people hurt me so much?*

All those things went through my mind at that young age. And I felt guilty about what I did. I was depressed. There were times that I didn't want even to leave my room because I felt so unloved.

I knew that my mother was never going to let me keep the babies, so I didn't even think about trying to keep them. That was non-negotiable. It was a cute idea to have a baby. But I lived in such a small town, that if people figured out that I was pregnant, it would have been disgraceful. At that age, if I were found out to be pregnant, the whole town would be talking about it.

My mother was protecting her reputation. She forced me to service her friends. *That* she had no problem with. But a pregnancy that was the result of her trafficking me... *this* would embarrass her.

I don't know if our small town already knew about her. The principal who she slept with lived in another town and would come in on a motorcycle every day and leave. I suppose there was a possibility that they didn't know about her.

I think the people in our town knew she used to sleep around with a lot of guys, but no one would ever dare to approach her about this. She used to go to the bars and drink with those men, but no one ever spoke about it, at least not in front of me. In her mind, maybe she thought nobody knew.

The much older man who would become my husband and the father of my children gave my mother a cow and some money. In exchange, she gave me to him to be his wife.

Why did I marry him? I was never in love with him, I didn't know what love was. He noticed me when I went with my father to Abuela Lili's to get palm branches one Easter when I was very young. He bargained with my mother for me. I was sold for the third time at 16 years old.

I didn't have a wedding. We got married in the city, in a lawyer's seedy office. My husband-to-be had his sister with him, and he had to get two strangers off the street to be our witnesses. The lawyer didn't care about how much older he was, or how young I was, as long as he got paid.

Any hopes I may have had that this situation might present an escape from my mother were quickly put to rest. Even though she had sold me off, I still had to live with my mother. I was still only 16 years old when my husband went back to the United States. I didn't go with him because he hadn't obtained the necessary travel documents for me.

I decided that I would go back to night school and earn my high school diploma. I thought if I got my diploma, maybe I could find a job, put away some money, and get out of there.

Once my husband left to go back to the States, everything went back to normal. By *normal,* I mean my mother allowed her "men friends" to have sex with me. It didn't matter to her that I was married.

I hate to say it, but I was wild in high school. My life was such a mess that it didn't seem to matter what I did. Nobody cared. Even my new husband left without me to go to the United States.

I met a guy I liked. He was a soccer player. l knew that nothing permanent could happen with him because I was already married to someone else.

The soccer player was nice. We went out a couple times, but I didn't sleep with him. I wanted him to think something that wasn't real. I wanted him to think I was good like other girls, and for him to respect me.

This was all behind my husband's back because he was in the United States. I was sleeping with guys—using them, pretending that I cared for them—even though I hated men for the way I had been used. I had been so betrayed by men and I wanted payback.

But I didn't want to sleep with the soccer player. We would go to the park and we had a 'girlfriend' and 'boyfriend' relationship. He didn't know anything about my life, my mother, or my husband in the U.S.

One day he invited me to go to his house, and I went. His mother was there, and everything was nice. This made me like him even more. He invited me to go to his house again, on another day after soccer practice. We got to his house but nobody was there this time.

"I want you to come to my room so I can show you some things I have."

When I went to his room, he pushed me on the bed and tried to force himself on me. I fought him, and I didn't allow him to do anything. I don't know why, exactly, but I didn't want it. I wanted him to believe that I was very different from who I was.

I remember running from his house. I had to cross the railroad tracks, and I jumped them. He ran after me, calling, "Sioni! Come back!" But I never even looked back.

I continued running until I got to a place where I felt safe. I never wanted to see him again. I didn't want to have sex with him and I wouldn't allow him to force himself on me. This was more than I knew how to handle, and I carried that memory through the rest of my time in school.

I became even more aggressive with men. I didn't care about anyone else. I was a very angry, person. It was almost as if I was getting revenge because of the men who hurt me when I was young. Like the time Chunches and I got revenge on that snake for killing our dog.

# Life's Promises

It was August of 1987, and I was 17 years old, when my husband came back from the U.S. He didn't stay long. And shortly after he left, I realized I was pregnant.

My pregnancy made my mother angrier than ever. Both my mother and now my brother hated me with a passion. I was accustomed to my mother's mistreatment, but I didn't understand Humberto's drastic change. It hurt me deeply. He wasn't acting like he was my 'Chunches' anymore.

It seemed like he was always angry. He would hit me every chance he got. Once, he kicked me in the back. I thought I would lose my baby. Looking back, I wonder if he was just afraid that I wouldn't care for him anymore when I had someone else to take care of.

When I tried to tell my father, he screamed at me and called me a liar and a troublemaker. So life hadn't changed much.

When I turned 18, I received my high school diploma. I was huge with my pregnancy at my graduation. I was the target of hurtful bullying because of this.

What should have been a happy day was painful because there was so much ugliness directed at me. People treated me as if I was second-rate because I was pregnant, but my husband left without me. They saw me as someone who didn't deserve respect. But I was still proud of myself.

When it was time to deliver my daughter, there was only one way for me to get to the hospital. Don Matias had the only vehicle in town, an old pick-up truck. He used it to operate a sort of taxi service. Blankets were put in the flatbed of the truck, and that's where I lay, by myself, for the 45-minute drive. The dirt road was rough with potholes at every turn, making it a miserable ride. Then I was left at the hospital, still alone.

The delivery ward was one huge room that could hold up to 30 women, all pushing and screaming at the same time. It was a terrible experience, especially when I was so young and without anyone to help me.

My labor lasted for a brutal *eight days*. The doctors didn't offer pain medication. They didn't consider a cesarean section for me either. Even as recently as 1989, when my time came, Costa Rica was still backward with medical care. The nurses offered only one solution when I said the pain was too much to bear, "Walk. Walk!"

My delivery was a nightmare. But Scheila was finally born, and I thought my heart would burst with love from the moment I saw her little face! She was *so* beautiful, and had the most striking blue eyes! I forgot about everything else when she looked at me!

Scheila's father saw her for the first time when she was about 6 months old. He was once again in Costa Rica, and brought her some clothes and a baby blue stroller.

He took me on a honeymoon by the ocean in Playa Jacob, where we stayed in a good hotel. It was the first time in my life that I had a vacation. It was a new experience to have people to wait on me! I had a very nice time staying in the hotel with the baby. He was very kind then.

He went back to the United States again, leaving the two of us behind. I enrolled at the University to study nursing. I was living in Oriente and school was very far away in Turrialba. Each morning, I would leave my house at 3 o'clock to make the bus at 4 o'clock, and arrive at school by 7 o'clock. Besides that, I was taking typing classes, in the opposite direction, in San Jose.

My sister-in-law would babysit Scheila. I didn't worry about Scheila being abused when it was my sister-in-law who took care of her. I would never leave her with my mother. It was a hectic time. But I was young, healthy and determined to find a way to take care of myself and my daughter.

My husband didn't come back again for over a year. During that time, my mother still allowed her men to use me for sex. She continued to allow Gilber to use me. I became pregnant again.

I was being used by so many men, that I had no idea which one of them had made me pregnant. Still, now that I had a child of my own, I wanted to keep this child too. My mother would not allow it. She beat me and dragged me to the city and once again she forced me to have an abortion.

I continued and then completed my nursing studies and earned my associate degree. My husband came back to Costa Rica when Scheila was 17 months old. As always, he soon left and returned to the States. Not long after that, I discovered that I was pregnant again.

When my mother found out about the pregnancy she was furious, as usual. She said she was taking me to the city and I was going to have an abortion. I was not to be allowed to have another baby.

I was married to the baby's father. But I think she was afraid that he might not ever come back from the States to get me. That would leave her stuck with me, along with my two children and without a father for them.

She tried to force me into another abortion, but I refused. This time, I couldn't bring myself to do it. I had already started my own family. I couldn't kill this innocent baby. Somehow, from somewhere, I found the strength. I let her know that if she wanted to kill this baby, she would have to kill *me* this time. And so, in 1991 my sweet baby boy was born.

My mother was so evil that she didn't know how to love and be a good mother. I wouldn't do that to my children. I set out to be the total opposite of my mother; to be very caring and loving to my children.

# Running The Race

When Scheila was about a year and a half old, we had to take a 45-minute long bus ride from our little town. People would bring every kind of animal on the bus, from a dog to a goat. On this day, there were so many people that the bus capacity was overflowing. There was no air conditioning, and people were hanging out the doors. The bus took dirt roads that left a thick dust covering every corner of the bus.

People would take this bus about once a week to go to the city to do their shopping. I had taken Scheila with me for her doctor's appointment, and also to do some errands. There was a huge bus station, with buses coming from all the surrounding towns. This bus stop was filled with long wooden benches where we would sit and visit while we were waiting for our bus to arrive.

Everybody knew everybody else, and while we were waiting, I was talking with friends. Sheila started crying, so I bought her a vanilla ice cream cone, which made her both happy and quiet!

I was sitting on the bench with a lot of other people who were also waiting for the bus. The bus came, I grabbed my stuff, and jumped on the bus.

About 10 minutes into the trip, somebody said, "Sioni? Where's Scheila?"

I couldn't believe it! Everybody started screaming at the bus driver to turn around. "Pipo, Pipo! Turn around! Sioni left her daughter at the bus stop!" Immediately he made a u-turn on that gravel road and went back to the bus station.

And there we found her, sitting right where I left her, still content and eating her ice cream!

By the time I was pregnant with my son, Humberto was already married and out of the house. He wasn't there to hurt me anymore, so my pregnancy progressed much easier this time.

Every year at Christmastime they have a fair in our pueblo. I went to this fair the day before my son was born, and even went on the Ferris wheel.

I felt a little pain while I was on the ride, but I ignored it. I was riding the Ferris wheel with my Papi and enjoying the time with him. This rare moment got all my attention. Plus, I didn't know that the baby was going to come the next day. We had no ultrasound machines or anything like that, so I had no way of knowing exactly when the baby would come.

We were living in the blue house then, with the latrine out back. On that day, I went out to the latrine and I felt a sharp pain in my lower back, but, again, I didn't think anything of it.

My father butchered a pig so that my mother could make tamales. Tamales are a favorite food in Costa Rica. My mother would make them for our family and give them as Christmas gifts. She had me make one of the deliveries to a place that was about a half hour walk away.

By the time I got to the house, when I had knocked on the door, I felt a huge pain. When the lady of the house opened the door, she asked if I was okay. "I hope you're not giving birth right here!"

"No, it's not time yet."

By the time I walked back to the house, I was having more and more contractions. By 8 pm, I was lying in bed with a sharper pain. But I was still traumatized by my daughter's birth, and I didn't want to go back to that abysmal hospital.

My mother said, "You'd better go to the hospital because you're not going to have that baby in this house." By 8:15 I couldn't take the pain anymore, so I decided I had to go. And again, Don Matias (and his pickup truck) was hired to take me to the hospital. This time I had my sister-in-law with me for the bumpy ride. She didn't stay with me, though, and returned to Oriente in the truck.

Immediately upon arrival, my water broke. The nurses took me right to the same delivery room where Scheila was born. The crowded room still offered no comfort, with women screaming in their labor. It was all natural childbirth, with no painkillers or epidurals. And once again, I was all alone. My husband was not there for the birth of either of his children.

When the nurse walked away, I couldn't take it anymore. I held my eyes shut tight, and I pushed so hard that I pushed the baby right out. I pulled him out myself and put him up on my chest. The nurse was shocked. "What did you do that for?"

"It hurt too much. I wanted this to be over!"

When I looked at the nurse's face, I realized that something was terribly wrong. Then I saw the umbilical cord was wrapped around the baby's neck and he was turning blue. She rushed us up to a room where there was a doctor. He immediately removed the cord, but the baby remained lifeless.

I was terrified! I thought my little baby was dead and that I was responsible. The doctor smacked the baby on the back and rear end but nothing happened. I held my breath and couldn't move. The doctor smacked him again and then a third time and suddenly Cheo began to wail. That screaming was the most beautiful sound I had ever heard!

The people in the labor room couldn't believe that I delivered my baby by myself. I was small, but I figured out how to take care of myself. I had already gone to nursing school by that time, so I had a little bit of confidence that I could do it.

Still, I was afraid that Cheo would not be a normal child after his difficult birth. Sometimes I feel horrified that if something had happened to him, it would have been because of what I did.

My mother didn't seem to like Scheila at the beginning because she was a girl. I shouldn't have been surprised, since she had favored my brother over me. Boys were valued more than girls. When Cheo was born, though, she started treating her granddaughter better.

My mother was always drinking, partying, or having sex, enjoying her life. She wasn't interested in the babies. She had not been a loving mother at all, so her lack of concern or care for her grandchildren was not a surprise to me.

Yet, my father was very close to my daughter. He would come home from work to be with her. Whatever he wouldn't do for me when I was a young girl, he did for my daughter in the two years we were there. It was so nice to listen to my dad when he sang to Scheila until she fell asleep.

When Cheo was about 8 days old, I had to bring him to the hospital for newborn tests. I wrapped him in a thick comforter. I had no baby carriage at that time; I had to carry him in my arms.

The hospital was on a hill. The way to get to the entrance was a staircase of about 60 concrete steps. You could stand at the bottom of the steps and look up, but all you would see would be more stairs. If you weren't in good shape you'd be quite tired by the time you made it to the top.

I was by myself again, with my newborn son on one arm, while Scheila was walking and holding my other hand. Before I started up the stairs, I situated the kids and everything I was carrying. I didn't want to have to stop along the way. I threw my son up on my shoulder and started up the steps.

When I was about halfway up the steps, I heard somebody from the bottom yelling up at me.

"Señora! Señora! You baby is here! Here on the ground crying!"

What happened was when I threw my son up on my shoulder, I didn't notice that he had slipped right out of the thick quilt! I left Scheila right there and ran down the stairs to him. Then I ran back up the stairs to get Scheila and then ran to the hospital to have him checked over. They assured me that everything was fine, but I was so scared!

When I told that story to my son, he played as if he was mad. He joked, "You know when you did that, you must've knocked some sense into me!"

I was able to get my associate degree in nursing while I was still in Costa Rica, but I never got to work as a nurse. I finally got my temporary green card and went to live in the United States.

I thought I was moving away from Costa Rica so that my children would never have to live with abuse. I thought I was moving to the United States to be with someone who was nice. When my husband and I were together in Costa Rica, I even thought he cared for me.

# Reaching The Goal

My husband was able to complete the paperwork needed for us to come to the United States in 1991. He bought airline tickets for the three of us, and I finally left Costa Rica, my mother and that desolate life behind me.

The night before we were to leave, I spoke to an older man I knew and arranged for him to take us to the airport. I had a little money saved and I offered him $20, which was a lot back then in that country.

He had to pick us up at 2:00 AM because the airport was three hours from my house. I was very relieved that his wife, Doña Rosa, came along with us. It made me feel safer to have her there and she offered a little help with the children.

I didn't speak much at all during the entire ride. I remember how very quiet it was in the car. Cheo and Scheila were sound asleep in that deep, serene way only innocents can sleep.

As we drove away from town, with everyone asleep and the car silent, I began to feel happy inside. I was finally getting free from that place. I imagined there would be better opportunities for the children and myself. I trusted that after reuniting with my husband, that we would have the family life I had always dreamed about. After all, he had been so kind on our honeymoon. I felt that all the pain and frustration of the past was over. I was leaving that all behind and beginning a new life.

I arrived in the United States with a toddler, an infant and five bags packed with everything we had. We landed in Miami, FL first, then we had a five-hour layover before our flight to Newark, NJ.

It was difficult for me to maneuver through the airport with two little ones. Scheila wanted to run and touch everything and it was a challenge trying to keep holding her hand. Then of course, with my other arm, I was carrying my infant son.

I didn't know how to speak a word in English. I didn't know that in Miami there were a lot of Latinos. In my mind, I thought all Americans were Caucasians who wouldn't know Spanish. I was tired, and hungry, I had to use the bathroom, and I didn't know how to get around the maze inside the airport.

My husband and his sister came to pick me up at Newark's airport. It was winter, and very cold. The children and I had only summer clothes. They brought two blankets to wrap the children in, and his sister had a heavy coat for me.

I was happy when I saw them. His sister has always been one of the nicest people. It was good for a little while, living with his sister in Trenton for a week or two, and then we moved to Bristol PA.

I was extremely excited. I was going to live the American dream. My husband, if not loving, was at least kind. I had my children and I thought I would live in a quiet home of my own.

About six months later, things started to go bad, and it seemed that I had stepped right back into the pit. This man became exactly like my mother.

The screaming increased. Oddly, I didn't mind the screaming much because that's the kind of home that I came from. I figured it was normal for him to get mad and I would make excuses for his behavior.

He started doing things to me that were vile. When I wondered why he was this way, I thought about his father. He was raised by his grandmother, not his parents. When his father came from Costa Rica to visit, things started to change. He changed how he acted toward me. I'm not sure if his father's visit had anything to do with it.

The apartment we lived in was empty except for a stove and a refrigerator. It had two bedrooms, but not any furniture. After a while, I got a few things from the Salvation Army. I never got any living room furniture. That was fine with me because it left the living room open, giving the children a good place to play.

One night he left us. There was no heat in the apartment. I don't know why there was no heat, but there wasn't, and we were sleeping on the floor. I kept Scheila and Cheo close in next to me, because I was afraid they would die, that they would freeze to death. I didn't sleep because I was afraid my children would die if I wasn't watching them carefully.

After that, my husband started coming and going whenever he wanted. The only relief I had was when he was gone. He did not "live" with us in a normal family way or for any length of time. When he was with us, if he was angry—and everything made him angry—he was violent and abusive.

Although I couldn't speak much English yet, he found me a job at Kmart as a warehouse worker. An Indian woman from our apartment complex watched the children while I worked. I didn't make much money, but I set aside few pennies from my paycheck whenever I could. I knew that I could get my small savings to grow if I kept at it.

After four years, I decided to try to buy my own house and leave my husband. I saved $100 to use as a down payment. I was naïve enough to think that my hard earned $100 would be plenty!

I walked into a real estate office and spoke to the women at the first desk. I told her with confidence that I wanted to buy a house.

We looked at some houses. After talking about prices, the woman asked how much I planned to use as a down payment on the loan. I told her with pride that I had set aside $100.

She looked at me in astonishment. She said, "You can't even buy a shed with only $100 down!"

I turned and walked away. I was completely disheartened.

Still, I refused to give up. I was desperate to get away from my husband. Not long after, I happened to meet a man who sold real estate out of his home. I told him how I wanted to buy a house but that I didn't have enough down payment.

But he said, "yes, you do!" I couldn't believe it; something was actually going to go right. I knew just what I was looking for and I was excited to have help.

He was true to his word, and he helped me with the whole process and I was able to purchase my first home. I'd never felt so proud of myself. It was a monumental achievement for me and a huge step forward for my family.

It was a small house in Beverly, NJ, but it felt like a castle to me. I was very happy. I was going to live peacefully and quietly there with my children.

Financially, things were very tough. I had to work long hours of overtime, leaving the kids with baby sitters. And although I was working all the time, I was having a hard time making ends meet.

Like so many other abused women, because of money problems, I made a desperate decision. I let my husband move back in with us. He convinced me that things would be good, and I convinced myself that it was worth the risk for the financial help. I would do this for the kids, to keep a roof over our heads.

He moved in, and happiness went right out the window. The physical, mental and emotional abuse grew and expanded into new horrors at every turn.

There were the times when he was out of control with anger. He would grab me by my hair, which has always been very long. He would pull me down the stairs by my hair, my head hitting *bump, bump, bump* down each of the stairs.

I had rescued a dog and taken it home as a pet for the children. Naturally, the puppy had an accident on the floor in the basement. So he dragged me down the stairs and rubbed my face into the filth and then proceeded to use my hair to "clean up" the mess. That type of abuse was more or less the routine for as long as we lived together.

It was very clear that I wasn't going to get by in the United States without knowing the language. I was determined to learn to speak English.

I created my own system to teach myself English. I started watching television – specifically the soap opera, *General Hospital*. I would listen to what they said, and then I'd repeat what I heard. I learned that Americans express a lot with their hands. That helped me to understand what they were talking about.

I started buying the newspaper to teach myself how to read. I have no idea what I was "reading" in that newspaper, but I did my best with what I could figure out!

My English improved over the years until finally, I was able to go to the local college for language classes. I was amazed that the professor was Russian. Here we were—all immigrants—trying to learn English from another foreigner!

One night in class, I raised my hand.

"Sir. I want to have a perfect accent."

"You weren't born in the United States. You will never have a perfect accent."

After that reply, I didn't see the point of trying to learn from this college class. Instead, I continued to improve my English with frequent conversations with native-born Americans.

I drove a beat-up car when I was young in Costa Rica, but I didn't have a driver's license. Now I was the mother of two kids and living in America. I was alone much of the time. I wondered, *What if my children needed to go to the hospital?* It was clear that I needed a driver's license.

I got one of the guide books the state provides for people to study for the written test. I saw the red sign with white letters and knew that meant to STOP. I learned that a dashed line down the middle of the road meant it was okay to pass another car. I still didn't know how to read a word of English, but I memorized all the pictures. I didn't even know the right place to put my name on the test, but I passed it, and I got my driver's license!

I had only been in the United States for a short time (my son was about 6 months old) when my husband left us the first time.

I was living in Bristol, PA at the time. I had to work two jobs to bring in money to pay my $363 per month rent, plus $70 for babysitting. What money was left over—and not much was left over—was used for food.

One night I arrived home around 11 PM, to find the babysitter crying and distraught.

My husband had forced his way into the apartment and had taken the children.

I immediately knew where they must be. He would have taken them to his sister's house in New Jersey. I called the police, but they said they couldn't help. The state of New Jersey was outside of their jurisdiction.

I jumped in my car and drove to his sister's house by myself. I knocked on the door, and his brother-in-law opened the door. Now, he's a big guy, but I pushed right past him to get to my two children, who were sleeping on the couch. He tried to stop me, but I was desperate.

"Don't you get in my way, or else!" I grabbed my children and put them in the car.

They had called the police, who arrived as I was leaving. I had a hard time trying to put together full sentences in English. Eventually, I was able to explain that my husband had taken my children away from me. Thankfully, one of them was a Puerto Rican who started speaking Spanish to me. Once he understood my explanation, he told me that he was only giving me a warning this time. He said that I should not make trouble like this again.

They lived in Trenton, a short trip across the border from Pennsylvania. As I crossed the bridge into Morrisville, PA I felt a surge of relief that they would not be able to do anything further. But as I brought my children home, I was still afraid that my husband would come back for them again.

After that, I cut back to one job so that I could be home at night in case he tried to take them again. That meant less money for everything—including food. It got to the point where the only thing I had in my house was bread, ham, cheese, and water. Often times I would not eat to make sure there was food for the children.

I was so desperate that I allowed my husband to sleep with me when he would come to visit the children. He used to come sometimes to be with me and would give me $20 to buy milk for our son. The only reason he would give me money is if I would sleep with him, so I would do it for my son. Then I got pregnant again.

But I used to sleep with other guys too, so they would also take care of us. I didn't know for sure whose baby it was. I was living by myself with two little kids, and I was afraid. I ended up going to an abortion clinic.

I could have had all these kids, but I when I was very young, my mother forced those abortions. The abortion that made the most impact on me was this one, where I went to the abortion clinic on my own. I felt like I would have done much better raising this third child But then again, I didn't have any means to support another child. I had to find forgiveness for myself after that.

After a time, I started being nice to my husband again. That's what you have to do to break the chain of fighting, or it will continue indefinitely. Someone has to be the first one to change things.

One morning he came to see the kids. He sat at the kitchen table I got from the Salvation Army, and I offered him something to eat or drink. When I opened the refrigerator, he could see that the only food inside was bread, some cheese, and a pitcher of water. This made him visibly upset, and I asked him what was wrong.

"I've just come from the Immigration Office. I told them you had drugs in the house."

"Why did you do that? You know that I don't do drugs and there are no drugs in this house."

"I wanted them to take the children away from you. I wanted them to send you back to Costa Rica, so I can have them."

He was right that they could deport me at any time. I was in the country legally, but I had only a temporary green card.

I didn't understand why he did this. Maybe it was because he wanted me, but I didn't want him. Maybe it was because he was a bad person. I don't know. But when I offered him something to eat and drink— even when we had so little food for ourselves—he suddenly understood how wrong he was. He swore that he would go right back to Immigration and explain to them that he had lied about me. But it was too late.

Immigration agents came to check my apartment to make sure everything was okay. They did a thorough investigation. There was no sign of drugs, and they concluded that what I told them was true, that I never used drugs. The case was dropped.

That's why I was determined to become an American citizen. I had to protect myself.

In two years I got my permanent green card. After that, I was required to pass the final citizenship test. I prepared by memorizing the Constitution of the United States! There were 100 questions on the test.

There was one question that I needed to answer in written form. The problem was that I didn't know how to write in English yet. I was worried and nervous, but the woman who gave me the test was very kind. She gave me a sentence that was easy enough for me to handle.

"I want you to write, 'I love my children.'"

I wrote it and I passed the test with a 95! I remember being so happy that I was screaming and jumping! It was a great achievement for me, and in 1995 I became an American citizen!

Now no one could threaten me with deportation ever again. I spent the next few years becoming more accustomed to life in the United States, and focused on building a good life for my children.

## *God Is My Help*

When Scheila was ten years old, and Cheo was eight, we lived in Browns Mill, NJ. One Sunday morning, I was driving with them to a park.

As I passed the barber shop where I would take my son for his haircuts, I noticed a church next door. The church was quite small.

It was a summer day and they didn't have an air conditioner so the windows and doors were wide open. This made it so we could hear the music coming from the church. Over the music was a familiar sound that brought me back to my childhood—the tambourine!

I decided to stop to check it out. When I got inside the church I realized it was a Spanish church. It felt so good to find a place where I didn't feel out of place with my accent. As I walked in with my young children, people said "hello" or "good morning" as if everything was normal. In the same way as when I first entered a church setting at 12 years old, they were warm and welcoming. The feeling was an incredible sense of joy.

The pastor was preaching in Spanish but it was hard for me to understand. This was a Puerto Rican church. They speak a very different Spanish than the Costa Rican Spanish I learned as a child.

As the service concluded, the pastor said a welcome to the visitors and turned his attention to me.

"Your name is…?"

"Sioni."

"Oh! God bless you and welcome to our church!"

After church, they were celebrating a birthday. The kids had cake and we all had a great time.

It's not easy for me to open up to new people. I didn't trust that they would like or accept me. But, I kept going to the church.

Every time I went, my husband would give me a hard time. He complained that everyone at the church was a hypocrite and was out to take our money. But I liked them, so I continued to go.

As time passed, I began to know the people who attended there. Eventually, I felt comfortable enough to ask them to pray for me and for my marriage. But I held back the details. I didn't trust enough yet to tell them the whole reason why I needed their prayers.

It's not uncommon that when you go to church, you find a little clique of people you're drawn to. You might find a person and say to yourself, *I like this lady, there's something nice about her.*

I didn't have any real friends there. But there was one lady I met, named

Guillermina. She started asking things about me and I opened up a little bit.

"I see you have a lot of bruises on your arms. What happened to you?"

Of course, I didn't want to tell her what was happening but started to explain a little at a time.

One day when we were praying, I started to cry. Guillermina was concerned about me and asked what was wrong. I finally explained to her I had the bruises because of my husband. I told her that he left marks on my arms when he had grabbed me. And then she noticed all the scratches and scars. I started to open up more to her and confided that my husband was beating me.

I told her about the ways that he was abusive to me, both physically and verbally. I described how he hit me, and he'd pull me and throw me against the wall. There were marks on my face because he used to scratch me with his nails. Some of those scars will be with me permanently.

I spoke with her every week after that. She gave me a bible, which I still have.

She said, "You can't continue to live with someone so cruel. It's not good for you, and it's not good for the children to see it."

One time, I invited my husband to come with me to the church, and he did. The children were all performing a skit at the beginning of the service. I thought it was important for him to be there for our kids. And for him too. But he lost his temper in an incident during the service.

I was keeping the beat of the music with two tambourines. I was so happy to have the instruments I loved so much, all to myself! The tambourines brought me back to the joy I felt when I played the tambourine as a child in Costa Rica. Back then, there weren't any instruments to speak of. Instead, everybody sang and played along with whatever they had in their hands. They all loved each other. Nobody cared if you weren't playing or singing perfectly. Nobody cared about anything but praising God.

But on this day, a woman came up to me and told me to stop playing the tambourines. She didn't like how I played them. I was devastated by this. But what happened next was worse still.

Right there in the church, my husband started to yell at the entire congregation. He said that the pastor was a thief, and was only there to take money from the congregation. He grabbed me by the arms, pulled me out of the church, tossed me in the car with the two kids and took off. I was so embarrassed that I didn't want to go back to their church ever again.

Guillermina saw with her own eyes that I was just barely surviving in a violent marriage. She said, "You don't deserve to be with a man like that. You're young and you have your whole future in front of you. Being a Christian doesn't mean you have to stay with a man who mistreats you. God doesn't want for His children to live that way. God loves you and wants the best for you."

Still, I stopped going to church for a long time.

Then I started to think that she could be right. I decided that after all these years I needed to make some changes for myself. I started to think about how I could leave this man.

# *Failure*

When I first came to the United States in the early '90s, I was busy getting my life together. I didn't have time to think about all the things they did to me back in Costa Rica.

Still, life in the U.S. was so difficult at the beginning that I thought maybe I should return to my old life in Costa Rica. It seemed like I had nothing in this new country that was worth staying for. But I was afraid to go back.

Then I returned for my first visit after four years of being away. I didn't want to spend much time with my mother and I avoided being with her as much as possible.

Instead, I took my children sightseeing, and traveled around the country.

We had a favorite park to visit, where trees had been clipped into fanciful animal-shaped topiaries. My mother said that she would like to see them too, so I this time I brought my parents along with us.

The kids and my father rode in the back, with the kids driving my father crazy, in the way young kids are apt to do. My mother rode in the front with me. We went up to the mountains, took some side trips, and went to dinner.

When it got to be nighttime, and we were coming down, I remember it was very foggy. I glanced at my mother beside me, and thought, *I don't like this woman. She was* not *nice to me.*

I thought I had forgiven her, but I'd only pushed the thoughts of her away. Keeping busy with the kids gave me a good reason not to deal with my feelings toward her.

If I had actually forgiven her, I would have wanted to spend time with her. I definitely wasn't there yet. I went back to the U.S., never telling her how I really felt.

It was all the same back at home. My husband would badger me and call me all sorts of names. He would say, "You're good for nothing. You're a whore and a bad mother. I hope you die and burn in hell."

He would curse at me and there was a lot of screaming. Screaming to the point where I would cover my ears and yell, "Shut up!"

He would repeat the same things over and over again, and that would drive me crazy. He used to put me down because I was born in the country, but I was from the mountains. He was born in the city, so he would call me "country girl." He meant a hillbilly, a hick. His purpose was to humiliate me.

By the time Cheo was 8 years old, he would go to his room and lock himself in when the fighting started. Scheila, at 10 years old, saw everything. She would yell at my husband to stop hitting me and to leave me alone.

This life with my husband was becoming increasingly impossible for me to endure. And now my children were being affected by it. My daughter was acting out and getting in trouble at both home and school. The school starting calling several times a week. They told me that she was sleeping in the classroom and fighting in the hallways.

I made the decision to take Scheila back to Costa Rica to live to see if a new start would help her to do better. I also took this as an opportunity to get away from a husband that I couldn't live with any longer.

My husband had an incredible way of twisting a situation to make himself look like the injured party. He convinced my son that I was leaving to be with another man.

Cheo didn't know if he should come with us or stay with his dad. It was hard for him to have to make a choice. In the end, he took his father's side and stayed in the U.S.

# Failure

When I moved back to Costa Rica I made sure that I was far away from my mother. I stayed in a small apartment, close to the mountains, about 5 hours from where my mother lived.

It was a beautiful, peaceful place. It had two small bedrooms, a little kitchen and living room, and a little bathroom. It had wood furniture—wood like the trees from a log home. Everything was made from logs and was very rustic.

Scheila and I began to get very close to each other. Our relationship grew better as the days and weeks passed. Our neighbors had horses and they allowed us to ride them. Scheila and I would ride deep into the mountains talking and singing together. I started to feel so peaceful and happy.

At first, Scheila went to a school that was a 45-minute drive to where the bus would pick her up to take her the rest of the way. Then she moved to a different school that was only 20 minutes away.

She had trouble in school because she didn't speak Spanish; she only spoke

English. She started acting out in the same ways she did while she was in the United States. I didn't know what to do next.

At the same time, I had the constant feeling that something was missing. I was missing my son. I so heartsick for him that I would sometimes burst into tears for no obvious reason.

I knew that if I was to stay in Costa Rica permanently, I would have to return to the U.S. and convince Cheo to move there with us.

*I'm hesitant to share this next part of my story with you. Like anyone, I hate the idea of being judged by people. Especially when they might not fully understand my situation. Still, being transparent about myself is important. It has to be that way so that you will understand more of my story. More than that, I cannot present myself to be anything other than what I am, even the parts that I'm not as proud of.*

# Failure

I never planned this, but during the six months that I was in Costa Rica, I met a man named Alexis. He offered me the moon and the sun. I thought it was a great thing because I came from such a broken and cruel relationship.

When I first arrived in Costa Rica, the town I settled in was in the midst of a festival. My mother was there because they were raising funds for the school. She was helping out in the kitchen selling and serving food.

I met Alexis through my mother. Alexis met my mother before I arrived in Costa Rica. He told me the day she introduced us, "Ah, your mother has spoken to me about you."

Alexis was attentive to me, and I was flirting with him. We danced a little bit and then had sodas and just chatted. We liked each other, so the next day I went back and we danced some more. Soon we started dating.

After some time, I started to see a pattern with this new man. He wasn't physically abusive and he never hit me. But he was very possessive. He wouldn't allow me to go out without him.

He knew how long it should take to travel from my house to his. He started watching how long it would take for me to get there.

When I arrived, he would want to know why I took so long. Even being five minutes later than he deemed necessary would cause him to demand to know what I had been doing. I began to feel like I had gone from one crazy man to another who was equally as crazy.

One night, Alexis started asking me questions and I decided not to answer him anymore. This was unacceptable to him. He took out the gun that he always kept in his waist band.

He put that gun to my head.

"I'm going to kill you."

When he saw that I was sufficiently terrified, he promised, "If you ever do this again, I'm going to kill you. I will never share you with someone else."

I was able to calm him down that night, telling him what he wanted to hear. But I said to myself, *I can't stay with this man a minute longer. I've got to leave immediately.*

The next day I packed our things while he was at work. I explained to Scheila's school that we had an emergency that required me to pull her out of school. I bought our tickets and flew back to the U.S.

Leaving Costa Rica saved me from dealing with the threats on my life from this man. I was happy to be back with both my children again.

But now I was back with their father.

My intentions were to live with him, but not to have any physical contact. My intentions were for him to help pay the bills until I could find a job. Without help with money, there would be no way for me to keep up with the mortgage and the car payments.

The screaming. The trouble.

All of it was back as if I'd never left it.

I was able to find a job as a maid in the hotel at the military base. It took some time, but eventually, I began to earn more money.

I was obsessed with becoming self-sufficient. I needed to be independent so that I could take care of my children in the way they deserved, and live in peace with them. I was determined that they would have a better life than I had. I would make sure that they had every possible opportunity to live good and fulfilling lives.

I didn't worry or even think about the past. I was entirely focused on the work I needed to do in the present. Somehow I knew that if I could get "now" right, the future would take care of itself.

Eventually, I was able to tell my husband that I could handle the bills without his help. I asked him to leave—permanently this time. He didn't want to go, but I insisted. Again, he got a lawyer for us. This time not for marriage, but for a divorce.

I didn't need a husband to give me money anymore. And I didn't need this man's, or any other man's wrath anymore.

# Overcome

"Sioni. You need to come right away. Your mother is dying."

It was a cold night in February, 2003, when I heard these words from my brother, Walter. Until that point, it had been a night like most other nights.

I was preparing dinner, which was always a little crazy, like it is for single moms everywhere. At the same time it was wonderful and fun. I was making their favorite chicken with rice and beans. We were together in my little kitchen with Scheila telling me all about her day.

Even though the place was tiny and I seemed to be working all the time, I felt peaceful. I had my kids with me and the three of us were safe.

The phone rang in the small hall located off the kitchen. Balancing the phone between my neck and shoulder, I continued cooking dinner.

"Hola!"

Walter never said *hello*, or *how are you?* He just blurted out that our mother was dying. I heard the words, but it took me a minute for the information to sink in. Everything came to a stop and the kitchen suddenly became silent. The kids sensed something was very wrong, and looked worried about what was to happen next.

I had only a year working at the Doughboy Inn on base. I wasn't sure what kind of reaction my supervisor would have to my short notice.

"Miss B? I need to leave the country. I need to go to Costa Rica because my mother is dying." Thankfully, she didn't give me a hard time, and I quickly made arrangements to fly to Costa Rica.

My flight out was that Friday. I didn't realize until I got to the airport that it was Valentine's Day. The gift shop was brightly decorated with red and pink hearts. Smiling couples passed by me, their happiness in stark contrast to my urgent business.

I had no idea what would happen later that day when I would reach Costa Rica. There wasn't a pink heart that would soothe my anxiety. All I knew is that I didn't have much time, and I needed to see my mother before she died. Before it was too late to fix what was broken between us.

No one was there to meet me at the airport when I arrived. I hired a cab to get to the hospital. The taxi driver looked through the rear view mirror and asked why I was crying. I told him that my mother was very ill, and she might be dying. He told me that he was very sorry to hear it. He said, "I know how important our mothers are to us."

I didn't know how to respond to his comment. My mother had never been important to me in the way he meant.

When I arrived at the hospital, Humberto was waiting for me outside.

"Are you going inside to see Mami?" I asked.

He said, "I don't need to see that woman. She's nothing to me."

"Humberto, you need to forgive your mother. Let go of the past so that she can die in peace."

And he said, "I will never forget what she did to me. I'm here only for my father, but I don't want to have anything to do with her."

As I approached the lobby, I could see that a lot of people were there, including my father. My father came toward me and I could see pain, sorrow, and confusion in his eyes. I now believe that for whatever the reason, he truly did care for my mother.

"Sioni, come quickly. Come upstairs. They're waiting for you to say goodbye to your mother. They're going to take her off life support."

I hurried to the room where my mother was. She didn't look like herself. She had lived through four heart attacks in only 48 hours. She had tubes all over her body, and her face was swollen from the medication. I cautiously approached her bed.

I knew that I had somehow come to a place of forgiveness for my mother. I felt it in my heart. But I had never told her.

It's possible to forgive someone, but not tell them, for whatever the reason. But they don't know they've been forgiven, and they don't receive your gift. I needed to let her know she was forgiven.

"Mami, can you hear me? I want you to know that I love you. I love you and I forgive you for everything that you did to me. Mami, I need you, please don't leave me, your grandchildren need you."

As I was telling her these things, she started jerking up and down as if she were trying to jump out of bed. I was afraid and couldn't tell what would happen next.

The doctors and the nurses ran to the room to find out what the commotion was all about. They told me, "Keep talking to your mother; she's coming back!"

There was something inside that made me bold. "Mami, I love you! I forgive you for what you did to me. Please stay with me!"

Just then, a priest approached the room. He said he was there to give her the Last Rites. We weren't Catholic, but I understood that this was a ritual he would perform because my mother was dying.

I said, "Please leave the room. You don't understand. My mother doesn't need the Last Rites. She needs Jesus, and that's all she needs."

He left.

The doctors repeated, "Keep talking to your Mami. See? She's coming back."

I kept talking to my mother, and she continued to lurch forward, trying to get herself up! When I left the room, she went back to the way she had been before I arrived.

The next day when I came again to the hospital to see her. "Mami, it's me. It's Sioni."

And she reacted the same way again! It went that way every day until the doctors decided they could safely take her off life support. After 8 days they removed the machines, and my mother was able to breathe on her own!

I had taken one month off from work. I wasn't sure of what kind of recovery she would have, but I wanted to show her love and compassion, and to be there for her.

The hospital was far away from my dad's town and he could only come on weekends. It was good that I was there to take care of her when he could not.

I went to be with her every day, all day, for that month. I would rub her fingers, and I would say, "Mami, if you can hear me, can you squish my fingers?"

Soon she was squishing my hand—with much strength—by herself! My mother couldn't talk while she was on the machines, but she would look at me like she was saying, *How could you forgive me? How could you be here for me?*

This wasn't a hospital like we have in the States. The nurses left the family to do any basic care for the patients. I bathed her, fed her, changed her clothes. Whatever it was she needed. And I showed her all the love I had to give, trying to catch up for lost time.

People would come to visit her, and I would step out for a short break. They left amazed at the miracle of my mother's recovery because the doctors had told them she was dying.

I stayed in a very nice hotel. It wasn't expensive, but it was only about two blocks away from the hospital. You could sit outside and see the city. I got up in the morning before I went to the hospital, and sat outside I watched the sunrise, and would have a cup of coffee. I could meditate and think in peace.

One day I was leaving the hospital to return to my hotel at about two o'clock that afternoon. The doctors were there to check my mother. She had been in intensive care, but now she was in a regular room because she was doing so well. As I was leaving, I saw my older brother, Walter.

I know he saw me. But he turned around and started walking away. I walked faster to catch up to him. Obviously, he didn't want to talk to me.

"Hold it! Come over here. Why won't you talk to me, Walter?" I looked him straight in the eye and said, "I forgave you many years ago. Look at me."

He looked at me, said nothing, and walked away.

Toward the end of the month, the doctors decided that everything with my mother's health was back to normal. They discharged her, and I took her home in a taxi. On the way there, she told me about her experience on that first day when I arrived at her bedside in the hospital.

She told me that she could hear me talking to her. But she couldn't reach me.

She felt like she was deep inside a black hole and she couldn't get out.

She said that heard me say, "I forgive you."

To her, this was like a hand reaching in to pull her out of that dark place.

My mother came back to us, because of the power of forgiveness.

# *Forgiveness*

The first time I really thought about forgiving my mother was in 2003 when my brother called me to come to her in the hospital.

All the years before, while I had been living in the United States, I thought I had forgiven her. I wasn't sure until she was in the hospital. I grabbed her hands and told her that I had already forgiven her.

Finally I was sure that I meant it. I know because of the difference in my attitude towards her.

When I visited in the years after, I genuinely cared for her. It was a joy to take her places, to walk together. I no longer felt sick about being with her.

Before, my mother had always been a pain in the neck! If I took her out to dinner, she was always making faces, and was very disagreeable with her complaining. Those things used to bother me a lot.

But after her stay in the hospital, even though she would still complain and be ungrateful, I felt sorry for her. I wanted to do the right thing for her.

If she didn't like the food a restaurant, I would say, "Oh Mami, check the menu and order something else." I felt compassion for her. In the past, I would have said, "Mami, please stop making those faces. Just be happy when we're together." When you're thinking about revenge, you haven't completely forgiven.

Forgiveness is so powerful when you forgive from your heart. I was even able to kiss her, which I had never done. We had always been distant with each other. I would never show her affection because of what she had done to me. But even this changed.

I'm glad that I was able to show her love and kindness in her lifetime. I don't regret that at all. She was finally able to know the daughter that she had never really cared about before.

Holding a grudge would have been easier. Few would blame me for wanting revenge for what she did to me. It would have been natural just to pretend that she no longer existed once I was free from her away from Costa Rica. All these things would be a natural response to her cruelty to me.

I don't choose to live that way, mainly because I am a Christian. As a part of being true to my faith, I learned to 'forgive my enemies' as Christ requires of us. To forgive just as we want to be forgiven ourselves.

Once I was living far enough away that she couldn't hurt me again, I could say that I forgave her because it was the Christian thing to do. No one would ever know whether or not this was an honest statement. Not even me. Trying to make a life for my children was enough for me to handle without trying to figure that one out.

I wasn't mature enough in my faith yet to recognize the signs that my forgiveness was incomplete. But the signs were there.

I didn't want to be anywhere near her. I didn't want my children around her. I was not going to make any intentional steps toward reconciling with her.

I was fine with things as they were.

Well, sort of fine, anyway. There was the guilt that I had because I knew things weren't really right. And there was the heaviness of the burden of carrying the pain of all the wrongs that were done to me.

What possible good would result if I did try? She was bound to reject me as she always had. Why would I set myself up to receive that pain again?

She was fine with things as they were.

The good that was possible was this: if I made a choice to forgive—and yes, it's a choice to forgive—I could be released from the pain and the anger. I could choose to stop looking for revenge for the wrongs done to me. I could let go of all that negativity and free up space in my head and my heart for the blessings in my life.

When I was traveling to Costa Rica to see my mother in the hospital, this choice was being worked out in my subconscious. Forgiveness was working subtly inside me.

But it came over me like a wave when I arrived at the hospital. I wanted to see her. I wanted to make sure she knew I forgave her and that I loved her. I wanted to be there for her.

I still had no idea of how she would react to me, but that didn't matter. I had made a choice to forgive, and as I walked to her bedside, it took permanent hold.

Notice that there was a chance that I wouldn't make it in time before she died. Or she might have rejected my forgiveness. This was of no consequence. It would have been disappointing, but I forgave her, no matter what her response might be.

This forgiving gave me the freedom to move forward with my life. This forgiving made me right with God.

*Bear with each other and forgive one
another if any of you has a grievance
against someone. Forgive as the Lord
forgave you.*

**Colossians 3:13**

# *Love For Me*

I met Richard in the middle of March in 2003. I had recently returned from the month in Costa Rica with my mother when she was in the hospital. I was working in the maid service at the Doughboy Inn, on base at Fort Dix, NJ.

Richard was in the Army and his unit was about to deploy to Iraq. They allowed the soldiers to have their families visit for the weekend before they were to leave. This was that weekend for Richard.

He was staying in the hotel I where I worked. I knocked on his room door.

"Maid service," I announced myself.

Richard opened the curtains at the window. It was almost the 11 o'clock check-out time but he asked if I could come back later.

"No problem."

I came back at about 12 o'clock to see if he was gone. By that time, he had already stripped the bed and had the bedding all ready for me to take. He had made a cup of coffee for himself and one for me.

We started talking and he asked me to have coffee with him. Our conversation was easy and friendly. He told me he was originally from New York, and that he was about to begin his tour in Iraq.

He asked me about which nearby restaurants would be best for seafood. I told him about some, and he asked if I would like to go to dinner with him sometime.

I turned him down, explaining that I didn't have time because I was raising my two children by myself. I wasn't ready to start a relationship with anybody. More importantly, I didn't want to bring any man into my children's lives right then.

Later, at the beginning of my lunch hour, I looked out to see him walking away. He was carrying his things in a small plastic bag, going to his barracks. I felt a little sorry for him. I jumped in my car and caught up with him. I asked him if he wanted a ride back to the base. He did, so I dropped him off at the barracks area.

There was a bunch of guys there, and I could hear them as they yelled after him, "Okay! Rodriguez!" Even though nothing had happened, they were sure that he was coming back from a romantic date with me. I didn't stick around to hear anything else!

Later I found out that he had stayed at the hotel because his family had planned to come to say goodbye to him. Unfortunately, they never showed up because his aunt's car broke down.

He was in the hotel anyway, and he had already paid for the night, so he stayed the night without them. It was much better than sleeping in the barracks. And he had noticed me working there.

He gave me his phone number. I put it away, but I had no intention of ever using it to call him. He came back a week later.

He said, "I gave you my phone number but you never called me!"

I lied and told him that I had lost his note. So he gave his number to me again, and I put it back in the very same basket that his number was tossed inside the first time. (I was kind of cute back then. In that basket, I had a collection of about 200 men's phone numbers, along with some love letters.)

After a while, he phoned me again.

"Why didn't you ever call me?"

"I lost your phone number again."

And he wrote it down for me again! Now he was starting to bother me, so I told him more plainly that I wasn't interested in dating him. I told him that he needed to stop chasing me. I think I might have accused him of stalking me!

All he said was, "Okay, then. Later for you!" And he disappeared. We didn't see or talk to each other for a long while after that.

It was about three months later when I saw him next. I was at the bowling alley with my children and one of my friends. The kids were having a great time bowling, and my friend and I were talking. I saw him come in with one of his friends. Curious, I stood up and looked at where he was sitting, but I acted as if I hadn't seen him.

"You see that brunette up there?" he said to his friend, Lopez. "You know, man, I chased that girl. She never called me back!"

Lopez encouraged him to go talk with me. Richard said, "Are you kidding me! I've already tried with her, I'm not going over there. I'm done with that girl."

Lopez pushed for Richard to try again. He said, "Look. All I've seen for months is camels. I don't want to hang out with you. The only person I want to see is a woman!

Richard stubbornly held his ground. "She's already got two girls over there and a boy. No way!"

Lopez harassed him so much that he finally agreed. Even then, he assured his buddy that it was only a "friendship that used to be, and that's all there will ever be."

Richard came and made small talk with us. He politely asked if we wanted anything to eat. Cheo was quick to speak up.

"Nachos and cheese!"

He got nachos for my son and a cold soda for me, and went back to sit with his friend. Lopez said, "I tell you what, if she comes back here, that means she likes you!"

He didn't believe I would, but I did! It wasn't long before I went to talk to Richard at his table. I was having a good time.

Later there was a soldier who made rude advances to my daughter. Richard came over and immediately calmed things down.

The other soldier may have backed down due to Richard's higher rank. But I'm convinced that it was because it was obvious that Richard was not going to allow anyone to disrespect us.

That was it for me—I was definitely attracted now! I've never felt protected like that before. This man was ready and willing to protect me—*and* my family!

He gave me his telephone number once again, and he walked away. He said to Lopez, "You're not going to believe me. This is the third time that I've given my number to this woman. Me, like a dummy."

I did call him though. "Hello. I was thinking about taking you up on your invitation to go out to dinner. It didn't turn out the way I expected though. He said he was sorry but he couldn't because he was in New York for training at the time.

So now I got annoyed. I remember making faces at the phone because I didn't believe his excuse. But I told him it was "no problem." He suggested that maybe we would go when he returned on Monday. I didn't really believe it would happen.

I discovered later that I lost his phone number for real this time! I looked for it everywhere and I couldn't find it! I decided the only thing to do was to go to every single barracks to ask for Richard Rodriguez until I could find him.

I was only 123 lbs and I had a nice figure. I was wearing a beautiful red dress with a big flower, and my high heels. I went looking for him.

When I got to the first barracks there was a soldier stationed downstairs, checking people in. I told him who I was looking for. He turned up the stairs and yelled, "Hey! Is anyone named Richard Rodriguez in here? There's a girl that's looking for him!"

I looked up the stairs and about 30 men came out from every single door in the hallway. One by one they all called out, "I'm Richard Rodriguez!" Each of them claimed to be my guy. I was so overwhelmed!

Finally, one of them said, "I *am* Richard Rodriguez!" But he had tattoos all over him, and he was most definitely not my Richard.

I said, "You're not the *right* Richard Rodriguez!" I ran down those stairs as fast as my high heels would let me go.

Then I thought to check where he worked. He had let me know that he worked in the publishing office that was across the street from the bowling alley. Sure enough, he was there. We started talking, and he was able to leave for lunch.

He asked me where I wanted to go, and I suggested a hamburger joint. I told him that I wanted something from the dollar menu. That's where I would go with my children so I knew that whole menu by heart. And that was our first date!

Not even a week later, I found a note from him on my car windshield that said, "I love you!" I thought he was crazy. How could he love me after knowing me for only a week!

But we started dating, and soon I fell in love with him too. I couldn't help but love him. He treated me better than I had ever been treated by anyone before.

I would be cleaning or working, and would catch myself smiling because I was thinking about him. I started to believe this man was the one man for me.

We were happy with just doing simple things together. Sometimes, after work, we would meet at a beautiful lake that was on the military base. We sat together on a park bench and watched the ducks, happy because we were together.

My feelings began to grow and deepen. These feelings were confusing for me at the beginning. Being in love was a new experience for me.

I remember asking one of my friends, "What is real love? How do you know when you're really in love with a man?"

She told me, "When you feel protected, safe, complete trust, and you can't remember what life was like before him. Then you're pretty close!"

After that conversation, I was sure that I was in love with Richard. One day I was in the hotel lunch room with friends, when Richard called me.

He said, "Honey, I'm sorry, but I'm on my way to New York. My orders have changed and they are sending me to Fort Drum this morning again for more training."

My heart sank, and I was suddenly very discouraged. It seemed like my past was catching up with me again, showing me that I was about to experience yet another major disappointment.

But during the next several weeks that he was away, I was able to go to see him. And he made the nine hour drive to see me every chance he could. It soon became evident that it was going to be different this time. I had finally found the happiness that was going to last.

About six months later, Richard came to meet me for Valentine's Day weekend. Richard was staying at the Doughboy Inn while he was in town. I went to work, knowing I would see him later, as usual.

One of his friends called me up to the family room the hotel kept for the servicemen to use for visits. When I opened the door to the room, I saw several of my friends at the tables, which were covered with red tablecloths. There was big cake that said,

*"I'm so in love with the girl from the Doughboy!"*

Now I didn't suspect that something was up. I thought everything was normal, and this was a nice party. I sat with my friends, talking and laughing, and having a good time.

I noticed Sergeant Hill, Richard's boss walk in. Then I saw Richard. He took out a piece of paper and started reading from it. He was nervous enough that he couldn't read much of what was written. He put the paper down, said a few things, and got down on one knee at my table.

Here's the thing, I had no idea what he was doing! I didn't understand at all. I couldn't figure out what was wrong with him that he would be kneeling down that way. This was not any kind of custom that I was familiar with.

He flipped his hand behind him, and Sgt Hill gave him a little box. He opened the box.

"Will you marry me?"

I was very confused about all this. I couldn't figure out what he was doing. Richard was confused because he didn't understand why I was hesitant.

Finally, I looked over at my friends, and asked them what I was supposed to say.

"Say, yes!"

I looked at him, and I said, "Yes!"

He put the ring on my finger and it was then that I finally realized that this was my engagement party!

Richard had arranged it all. He had one of my friends order the cake, and decorate the room. This generous man did it all in secret to be a surprise for me!

# Tough Decisions

My children's father didn't want me to marry someone else. After he found out I was dating Richard, he started making trouble for us. There were even a couple of nights that he tried to get himself into my bedroom by picking the lock.

I didn't want to be a divorced woman, and I didn't want my children not to have their father with us. But this was not a man who I could remain married to, both for my physical and my mental well-being. I needed to be no longer married to this man.

It was quite the opposite with Richard and I. We loved each other and he wanted nothing more than to protect me. He suggested that we should live together, even though we weren't married yet. He thought that we could have a good life together.

He wanted the children to live with us, as well. Scheila and I moved in with Richard in December of 2003, although Cheo did not.

Both of the children had a hard time dealing with the idea of leaving their home. Like all kids, no matter what, they didn't want their family separated.

They were both bitter and angry and showed it in different ways. Scheila began to get into trouble. Cheo refused to leave his father.

I don't know if his father threatened Cheo if he were to leave, or if he was made to feel guilty. But Cheo wouldn't leave our old home. His father would say, "Oh, so you're going to leave me! A son shouldn't leave his father."

Scheila was very disrespectful to me, to her teachers, and to pretty much anyone with authority. This brought a lot of stress to us as a couple. I was having a difficult time coping with all of it.

At one point, Scheila took the car and was in an accident. This was a very tough situation and she decided to go to live with her father afterward. I was feeling stuck between Richard and Scheila. I went through some times of deep depression after she left.

Richard and I fought almost every day. I tried many times to pack my stuff and leave. I was confused and my emotions were all jumbled up. I loved him but I also hated him. I regretted being with him, but then I wanted to stay. Ours was a very dysfunctional home.

The trouble was, I didn't understand why I couldn't be happy. I've never been happy for any extended length of time.

I was going through a lot of things. I thought, I had a terrible childhood, and now I have to live this kind of painful life. I just want to be happy, but there doesn't seem to be any happiness for me in this life.

Eventually, I went to a psychologist, who started me on medication to help me calm down. I didn't want to take it. I used to say, "Medication is for crazy people."

Therapy started pulling many long-forgotten memories out of me. The more I remembered, the more depressed I became. I would cry for five hours at a time. It was common for me to be up all night crying but still make it to my job the next day.

For the next three ·years, I saw my children only on the weekend. I tried to convince them to come to live with me. My son didn't want to and at that time, my daughter was angry with Richard.

It was very difficult for me to go see my children in the house that I used to live in with them. Now their father was living with them in that house and I was the outsider. Every time I drove to my old place, I felt like I had failed them.

The medicine didn't help me. Most of the time I would flush the tablets down the toilet, rather than take them. I tried the medications off and on for about a month or two, but more "off" than "on."

Talking to the psychologist opened all the old wounds. They gave me more reason to hate men. I started to accuse and blame

Richard. I thought about all the damage men had done to me. It seemed now I had this new man who was doing the same thing as the others did to me. I was convinced that all he would ever do is to hurt me.

That was never true. Richard has always loved me and he's only wanted to help me in every way. Like the way he didn't allow my daughter to act out and make problems for all of us. This was not to hurt her, but to both teach her and protect me from hurt. I wasn't able to see that at the time.

I wrongly thought he didn't want my children with us. I couldn't stop these thoughts. I was angry and argumentative. Sometimes I would yell. Even though I am very small in stature, I was ready to fight to protect myself and my children.

I was so confused by my emotions, that I was unfair to the one man who would look out for me. It was because I was afraid and discouraged. I felt like I was running a race, but I wasn't getting anywhere.

Richard and I sought help from our pastor. He explained to us that we should not be living together before we were married. We decided to get married at the courthouse as soon as possible. On April 6, 2005 we were quietly married by a judge.

Right afterward, in the parking lot outside the courthouse, Richard told me, "I want you to have a real wedding. The wedding of your dreams. The wedding you never had. To get married at the church and have the people you love and your friends there."

We were legally married, and I had been making preparations for our church wedding. I should have been happy. But without my children with me, I was under more stress than I could handle.

I laid out my wedding dress and got things ready in my apartment. Richard was working and I called him. It was only about noon, but I asked him to come back home.

He said, "I can't. I have to work."

"Richard, I'm going to die, I'm going to kill myself."

I put my wedding dress on, and I got on the couch. I was going to take a bottle of pills. This was the third time that I had felt so helpless that I could kill myself.

I had been going to church, but sometimes you can go to church and it doesn't mean anything. I was going to church with Richard, but with all the problems we had, even at church, I could never seem to find peace.

I could hear over the phone how desperate he was. He was too far away to stop me.

"Sioni! Sioni, don't do it!"

But I was determined to end my life. I was too tired to go on. I felt like I was bringing too much trouble to the people around me.

I took the bottle of pills, and I started taking them one by one. I took 5 or 6 or maybe 7 pills before I realized what I was doing and that I needed to stop. I didn't take any more.

What made me stop was thinking about my kids. I couldn't bear the thought of leaving them without a mother, so I stopped taking those pills.

I don't remember what happened after Richard got home, but I didn't go to the hospital. Richard took care of me.

Richard stayed with me. He knew everything about me, and he knew all about my past. But still he decided that our love was worth the work to get through this.

I am eternally grateful that Richard was there for me. He helped me to remember what was important in life.

## *Love, Love, Love*

I was able to plan every detail of the exact church wedding celebration that I had dreamed of. Our wedding was held in a beautiful military chapel. It was very exciting. Finally I was marrying the one man in my life who I really wanted.

Our wedding day was June 11, 2005. The night before, we stayed in a hotel. Richard had a room with the guys and I stayed in a room with my girls. I spent that night arranging the flowers. I was very happy about how everything was coming together.

On our wedding day, all the men left first to go to the chapel. My bridesmaids and I waited for the arrival of the limousine. I was anxious, but I was very happy. I felt like I must be the most beautiful bride in the world in my beautiful white dress and white gloves. I felt especially beautiful because of the long veil I had made myself.

The limo drove in at the front of the hotel. This was the same hotel where Richard and I met, where we got engaged, and where we were going to spend our first night after the wedding.

All my bridesmaids ran to get in for the ride to the chapel. I was the last to leave the room. That's when it happened.

The door closed, but my veil was caught on the other side because it was so long! It was a disaster because the veil was stuck inside and we couldn't find the maid to open the door!

I could hear the bells from the chapel ringing. I was very nervous! The wedding was scheduled to start at 2, and it was 2:15, and we could still not find the maid service to open the door.

At 2:30 the maid finally came to open the door and I was free! We got into the limo as fast as we could. And as soon as the driver opened the door to let us out, we started running to get to the chapel!

No one who was waiting for the wedding to start knew what was going on. Not even Richard. Everyone was wondering if I was ever going to show up for the wedding. I was 30 minutes late.

But once I got there, everything was just as it should be. This was my first real wedding. It was at a church, with my friends and loved ones there to celebrate the day.

The men in the bridal party were soldiers, so handsome in their dress uniforms. Even Sergeant Hill, the man who held the ring at the engagement party, was there.

The ceremony was performed by a Colonel, also in uniform. All my friends were in the front of the church. Cheo was 13 years old, and he was the man who walked me down the aisle. He and the ring bearer were perfect in their white tuxedos and bow ties. I had two flower girls, bridesmaids, including Scheila, and a maid of honor.

There was a pipe organ that began to play as I reached the aisle.

When Richard saw that I was finally there, he just smiled. He was so happy that I was going to marry him. My son walked me down the aisle, kissed me on the cheek and gave me to Richard.

On the way out after the ceremony, everyone threw a mix of rice and rose petals. I looked around and I couldn't believe it. This was my special day. My wedding in a white dress!

The reception was at the club on base. When we walked in, they announced us for the first time as Mr. and Mrs. Rodriguez. I immediately thought of another wedding that we had gone to in Queens.

I had been filled with jealousy when I heard the announcement of their names as husband and wife. I had thought, *Why can't I have a wedding like that? I'll never get married, there's nobody who will marry someone like me.*

Now on my wedding day, I was ecstatic! Richard was going to stay and we were going to be happy.

The courthouse wedding was legal enough. But everything changed on the day that Richard and I were married in the church.

All I could think was, *I can't believe it! I've had my church wedding! I'm at my reception with all my friends, and I've just married the man of my dreams!*

We went on our honeymoon to Costa Rica. That was when Richard met my family for the first time.

❁

Christians strive to resist evil so that we can enjoy a close, personal relationship with God. Fasting is one of the ways we develop the focus required to maintain this relationship. This is a time when we will abstain from what we would normally indulge in, often food. This helps us by reminding us to turn to God for our sustenance; to live by His plan for us.

When we arrived in Costa Rica, Richard was fasting. He did this because he was agitated over the things he had heard about my parents. He was searching for God's guidance on meeting my family, the people who had been so cruel to me.

I got upset. I felt hurt over his fasting because I didn't see it in a spiritual way. I thought, *Who do you think you are, fasting to disrespect my parents?*

Now I can understand why he fasted. It was because he wanted to be calm enough to meet these people that he didn't like before he ever met them.

My parents lived in Pejibaye, having long since moved out of Oriente. In fact, Oriente doesn't exist anymore. We had to drive over five hours from the hotel to get to their home.

When we arrived, I went inside alone. I said to my mother, "My husband is in the car waiting to come up. If he's not welcome here we won't stay. I won't stay here unless he does."

She agreed, and we brought him upstairs. My mother accepted Richard, and he accepted her. Now my husband says that it was the fasting that broke the anger he was holding.

On the way there, he told me that he wasn't going to stay. He had planned on only going in to say "hello" and then we would leave. But something happened once we got there. We started talking, and all the angriness was gone. The talk went well enough so that I ventured to ask my mother about my younger brother. She said that Humberto wanted to come see us, but we were leaving too soon.

It was Richard who decided. "If Humberto is coming, then we'll stay here." So we stayed with my parents for three days until he came. I wasn't sure that I could trust it yet, but it was almost as if we were a normal, happy family.

For the rest of our honeymoon, we did a tour to see every single place that I had ever been. I went back to Oriente even though there was nobody there. We saw the school. We went to the places where I spent my childhood. It brought me back to my past. We took pictures of it all.

We walked in many places where there was a lot of pain for me. But I also saw what I liked there. Places where I played with Chunches and my friends. I had mixed feelings. I would remember something happening to me in one place. But in another place, I would say, "Aw, look! This is where I used to be with my friends."

At first, after we got married, the dysfunction was still the same. But then things started to change. My daughter was grown and had moved out on her own, and my son still lived with his father. Richard and I moved to a nice house that we bought in New Jersey.

We went to Puerto Rico in 2006, and we brought Cheo with us. While we were there,

Richard asked him, " Cheo, would you like to move in with us? Let's try and see if you like it. And if you don't you can go back to live with your father."

Cheo agreed and moved in with us and started going to high school in Jefferson. Things started changing for me then. I was very happy because now I had my son living with me. Cheo never left. He stayed with me for four years until he graduated from high school.

# *Discouraged*

While Richard, the children and I were learning how to be a family at home in the U.S., there were other things happening with my family back in Costa Rica.

After my month taking care of my mother, I had to return home to my job, my children, and my life. I didn't go back to visit for a couple of years and when I did, Walter completely avoided seeing me.

My mother only lived three houses away from him. You could see his house from her front porch. In fact, to get to his house, Walter would have to walk past our mother's house. If I was on the porch with her, he would cross to the other side of the street as he passed. I knew he couldn't face me because he felt shame for what he had done to me.

I did see his wife. I visited his home each day of my visit. I enjoyed speaking to my sister-in-law and getting to know my nieces.

One day she said, "Sioni, will you pray for your brother? He is so depressed every time you come here that he locks himself up in his room."

She had no idea what the reason was for his behavior. I told her that I would pray for him, but I didn't tell her that I knew the reason for his guilt.

I discovered something else when I visited Costa Rica. Humberto still held the anger toward me that started when I was pregnant with my daughter.

When we were younger we never talked about the things he saw and the things that happened to us. Although we were both sexually molested as children, we've never talked about it together.

This is the brother who stood up for me the night Gilber came to my room and I was willing to end my life. I can't make sense of the reason why he changed so much toward me. He doesn't have a relationship with Walter, either. They barely speak to each other.

Apparently, Humberto still has to deal with the issues caused by the treatment we received as children. I wish that I could help him to come to terms with all the anger he holds inside. I've tried many times to reach out to him and bring back the close relationship we once enjoyed.

I pray that our relationship will be restored someday soon. I have not changed in how much I love my *Chunches*.

Mami lived until the year 2014. My sister-in-law was crying when she described what happened when she died. My mother called my name. She raised her hands and motioned to the watch that she wore. She cried, "For Sioni!"

When I went to Costa Rica on the day of her funeral, my sister-in-law gave me the watch that my mother left to me. She said, "Sioni, your mother gave me this to give to you before she passed away. She said this watch is for you, and I want to make sure you have it so that you can keep it for the rest of your life."

I know that my mother cared for me because in her last moments she called my name. I don't often think or talk about it, but I am consoled because of her gesture. Instead of calling for her two sons, she called for me.

I'm glad that I never told her how awful she was. I only wanted for her to see Christ in me. I don't regret it at all. I'm happy that we were able to repair our relationship before she died.

After my mother passed away, I found myself sitting in the church alone. I had such mixed feelings. I was mourning that my mother had died. But I was also in mourning for my childhood, and that I had never experienced being raised by a real mother.

I promised myself that I would bury the pain of all the things that she did to me, there in the ground with her body. I chose to let the past go.

As I was sitting there, I felt someone come near to me. It was someone different— not my husband. I turned around and it was my brother, Walter. He was crying and asking me to forgive him.

"Sister, please forgive me for what I've done. Our mother has passed away, and I want to get my life back now."

I looked at him right in the eye, and I said, "Walter, I forgave you a long time ago. I love you; you're my brother."

Humberto got very upset with me at our mother's funeral. He blamed her death on me. He said when our mother was very sick, I didn't come to see her right away.

Every time I called my family, I asked how she was, but they didn't tell me how ill she was. They said she's going to be okay, even though she was actually dying. I didn't know my mother was asking for me before she died.

In the small, rural towns of Costa Rica, we didn't take people to the funeral home. The body was brought to the family's home. Visitation was in the living room and everyone paid their respects there. Richard and I arrived around midnight on the day my mother died.

Humberto was there. He started screaming in front of everybody and accused me of neglecting our mother. "What the heck are you doing here? You shouldn't be here! Mami died and you weren't even here for her!"

I was speechless. I was completely shocked and couldn't believe what I was hearing. These horrible words, shouted at me with so much hatred, hit me like stones. I sat in disbelief, I couldn't say anything.

This is the guy who hated her so much that he couldn't come into her hospital room when we thought she was dying. This was the brother who said she was no mother to anyone and he couldn't bear to have anything to do with her. It was so strange to hear him say these things. All I could manage to say was, "What's wrong with you?"

Of course, Richard stepped in immediately to protect me. "Hey! Who do you think you are speaking to? Don't you dare disrespect my wife! You don't have any idea what we just went through to get here this quickly, coming from another country." As soon as he was confronted, Humberto was silent and walked away.

Since our mother died, Humberto has not spoken to me. I went back to Costa Rica a few months later, in June, to see our father. I called Humberto a couple times to suggest that we should get together, but he never returned my calls. I guess he still has to come to terms with his own feelings.

Oddly enough, it is Walter who wants to be my brother now. The man who locked himself in his room to avoid looking at me wants a family relationship. And the close brother of my childhood wants nothing to do with me.

Sometimes life is full of contradictions.

The next day after my mother passed, the whole family went to dinner. That's when I found out I had a sister I had never known about, and nieces and nephews too.

I had never had an experience like that, being all together with everybody. I felt somewhat out of place because I had never met this part of my family. Still, I enjoyed the time we spent together very much.

# *Let Go*

There were many people at my mother's funeral. One was Lila, the woman my mother had sold me to when I was a 9 year old. She offered her condolences as if everything had been normal between us.

Richard asked if anyone was there who had hurt me. A lot of men who had slept with my mother, had slept with me too, and some of them were there. I told him that there wasn't, but there were.

The men at the funeral didn't know what I looked like as an adult. Maybe they didn't recognize me. But I remembered them. I remembered their faces. The men at the funeral must have remembered that they abused the daughter of the woman being buried that day.

I looked at one, but I didn't want to make eye contact with him. I actually felt chained to my seat because they were there. It was weird. Geraldo, Jorge, Reinaldo, Franklin... in all, there were four of them.

A man walked up to give his condolences. I saw that it was one of them. I was disgusted. I didn't want him to touch me. I gave him a warning stare.

"Get *away* from me."

I hoped that no one had seen me talking to him.

Another came up to me and hugged me hard. "I'm sorry that your mother is dead."

But you hurt me when I was young. And you have the nerve to hug me now? I can't believe that I'm looking at your face, after what you did to me.

I forced myself to push everything else to the side. It wasn't easy but it was my mother's funeral, not a place for a confrontation. I knew what would happen if I told Richard they were there. I didn't want to disrupt the funeral in any way.

Funerals in Costa Rica are different than in the United States. The pallbearers sometimes have to walk long distances with the casket on their shoulders. Most of the time the people carrying the casket are members of the family.

My mother's pallbearers were my two brothers, my dad, my husband and two nephews. They went right past my mother's house for a mile or two to get to the cemetery. I did not walk. I was in a car with my niece, driving in the procession, right behind the casket.

It was a very hot sunny day. All the women were dressed in black, most carried an umbrella. I wore a beautiful black dress, shoes, and hat.

I drove very slowly, and that's when I made eye contact with one of the men. I immediately turned away. I didn't want him to make the connection between me as a little girl, and now as an adult. It made me feel very uncomfortable.

Once we got to the cemetery, we had to take the casket up a little hill before setting it down in a little enclosure. As I went up the steps, I felt somebody close to me. I looked and it was another one of them. He looked like he wanted to talk to me. I walked quickly ahead to avoid talking to him.

All this time, Richard was carrying the casket, so he didn't know what was happening. I didn't want to talk to or interact with these men. But internally, I said to them, *I am choosing to forgive you. I need to move on with my life.*

Forgiveness was happening at that church, right there during my mother's funeral.

After the funeral was done, everyone came to my father's house. It was such an uncomfortable feeling to be around those people. It was like I belonged there, but I didn't really belong there.

In my country, the women cook food for all the people attending the funeral. While we were eating, a man came up to me. It was one of the four that I had recognized. I put my plate in the kitchen and walked away. Richard saw this and said, "If there is anybody here who did anything to you, please tell me."

"No, Richard, there's nobody here. Just let it go." I didn't want Richard to find out they were there. I didn't want to make a scene, and I knew Richard would want to make something of it. This day was not about me; the only thing that mattered today was my mother's funeral. I felt that I had to put my feelings aside and let it go and move on.

Sometimes Richard is too overprotective, and that can be quite overwhelming. But he understood why I didn't tell him about the men at the funeral.

He understood that I wanted to stand up for myself, that I'm not a little girl anymore. I won't let them hurt me now. If someone tried to do this to me now, or tried to do it to my granddaughter, I would have no problem making sure they were sent to jail for it. Now, I know how to defend myself and my children.

My mother passed away in December. In June, six months later we went to visit my 78-year-old father for the first time after her death. We were surprised to find that he already had a girlfriend by then. He's dating and having the best time in his life enjoying his last years with this 80-year-old lady.

It seemed to me that my father was a victim of my mother too. I never blamed him for what happened to me. Still, my father beat me cruelly when I was young.

I felt that my father was a little bit better than Walter or my mother, I'm not sure why. I suppose it seemed like he was all I had. I never thought about having to forgive my father.

To be honest, my father in 25 years has never told me once that he was sorry. He never wrote me a letter, he has never been the one to reach out to get in touch with me.

I call him once a month. And every time I call him, he complains that I don't call him. He'll say, "You forgot about your Father." In the meantime, he's not calling me.

I tell him the same thing he tells me, that if I die he's never going to know because he won't call me to find out. I'm not bold enough to tell him how much this bothers me, I'm not sure why I can't talk to him about this. I suppose it's because we've never talked about any of the ways that he's hurt me.

He's 78 and he's not going to change. He's happy with his new lady, and that's simply the way it is.

He was very cruel to me when I was a child. It's as if Papi was under some kind of bondage then, because I know he has a good heart. I don't think he wanted to hurt me, it was my mother telling him to do it. She'd say, "Do it! You have to!"

It seems that my father was as much a victim as I was. I remember how cruel my mother was to him, how she used to treat him like garbage. My father lived in the same house where my mother used to sleep with other men. A normal person wouldn't do something like that.

Yet he was always there for her. Until the day she died, he would do everything for her, like cooking, cleaning and anything else. She would make fun of him, disrespecting him, treating him like a nobody. So I always saw him as a victim too.

When I came to know Christ when I was 12, we used to go to church together. He and I used to walk for hours together in the forest on our way to services. He gave his life to Christ back then.

But he stopped going to the church right after I was taken to the city because my mother forbade him to go anymore.

Even when I was older and I would visit, I would say, "Papi, how come you're not going to church?"

He would say, "No, no. You know your mother would be very upset." So even though he loved to go to church, he never went until after my mother died.

That's where he met this woman who he's in love with now. I spoke with him last week. He said, "You know, Sioni? I am happy in my life now. Your mother was so mean to me. But now I feel like a free man. I know that somebody cares for me and it's for real this time."

I was glad to hear that from him because he was never happy. He was a miserable man. But now he's happy and he's going to church. Now, finally, he has a good life.

## *Peace In My Mind*

**B**ack when I first came to the States, I had God in my life. I thought that I had forgiven my mother. But it wasn't until I saw her in person that I recognized that there was still something missing.

I had forgiven her in my mind, but not in my heart. I was still carrying the burden of hurt from being unwanted and unloved by my mother, as a child and as a woman.

When I saw her, though, things changed. She was in that hospital bed, weak and unresponsive. That made me realize that my love for my mother was greater than the pain that I felt.

It was the same with my brother, Walter. That day, in the chapel when he asked for my forgiveness, it I felt like it changed how broken I was. It was as if my mother's death brought him closer to me.

I've gone back to see Walter a couple times since my mother died. We've been able to talk and have dinner together with our spouses.

We don't talk about the past, though. His wife doesn't know anything about what he did to me. I thought it was not necessary to talk about that anymore. No one else should be hurt by our past.

Richard knows about what my brother did, and it's been very hard for Richard to look at Walter's face and smile. But Richard has worked it out and has been able to forgive him too.

I don't feel any bitterness any more. I can look at him and not even think about the things he did to me. I have made myself available to forgive him and not dwell on what he did to me.

For years and years, until my mother died, we were chained to the past. When she passed away, it was finally time to break every chain and Walter made it right with me. I accepted his apology because he was genuinely sorry, asking me to forgive him.

I accepted it when he apologized that day. I had forgiven him before, but I hadn't clearly said, "I forgive you and I love you." But I did on that day.

I believe in God. My knowledge of how much He loves us, even though we don't deserve it, made me see that I can choose to forgive. I could finally let the hurt go, and just love my mother and my brother as my family. I had moved on in my life.

Forgiveness is a decision, not an emotion. It is not about how you are feeling at any given moment. I made the decision to forgive those who hurt me. Not because I've forgotten the bad things that were done to me. I have forgiven because I did not want to carry the weight of bitterness and anger within me.

Seeing my mother in her hospital bed, allowed me to reaffirm that she could no longer control me. I made a clear choice. I allowed my forgiveness to evolve into a full reconciliation.

Forgiveness doesn't always include a reconciliation. Sometimes the person who wronged you will have passed away or is otherwise out of reach to you. Sometimes this person has no idea of how they hurt you, and they continue their life as if nothing has happened.

You can still choose to forgive them. Perhaps they'll never know it. But you will. And your burden will be lighter for it.

At my mother's funeral, I needed to keep a distance from the men who had harmed me. I wasn't looking to make them apologize, especially if it wasn't sincere. No, the risk of making things even worse was too great to begin a conversation about the wrong they had done.

Yet I chose to forgive their crimes against me so that I could finally be free of the pain.

With my mother and my brother, it was different. Reconciling was not only for their benefit, although I'm sure they felt better because of it. I made peace with them for my benefit.

I believe that since I accepted Christ as my Savior, that His Spirit dwells within me. That means that I must try to keep myself as free from strife as I can. To show the love of Christ to others, I need to have this love inside me.

So I forgave my mother and my brother, and I reconciled with them. I no longer agonize over past wrongs. Instead, I choose to create a meaningful future for my family and myself.

# Victory

After I returned from Costa Rica with Scheila, I put her in private school. I hoped that the discipline there would help teach her some self-control. Instead, she continued to act out and get herself into trouble.

She was a young girl who was trying to deal with a lot of confusion. I understood from experience how she was hurting and using anger to deal with her pain. I knew that she needed something that would help her focus and build some structure in her life.

I found a program in Fort Dix, NJ called *The New Jersey Youth Challenge.* This program is for teenagers who dropped out of high school and who need discipline. The goal is to help them to earn their high school diploma. It was high school, only it was operated similarly to a military boot camp. Her application to the program was accepted.

I often went to visit her there. And each time I went I had to beg her to stay. She kept insisting that she wanted to quit. Scheila has a mind of her own, and she didn't want to compromise on anything.

Somehow she remained in the program and graduated in six months. After she grew accustomed to it, she actually liked the military regimen.

When she graduated, she decided to join the Army. She was still a minor at 17 years old, so I had to authorize her enlistment. She completed her basic training without problems. She received orders to report to duty at Fort Lewis in Washington state.

December 14, 2007, is a date that will be forever burned into my brain. I was sitting down at my desk at work when I got a phone call from Pierce County Jail. I thought it was a wrong number. No one that I knew would be calling me from jail so I hung up the phone. Immediately the phone rang again. I picked up and the male voice said the call was from Pierce County Correctional Facility. "Would you accept a collect call from Scheila?"

I was still a little confused, but I accepted the charges. The first thing I heard was Scheila.

"It's me. I'm in jail."

For a moment I thought that my heart had left my body. To say I was stunned would be putting it mildly. I was reeling with confusion. She didn't give me details. She only said she had gotten into some trouble and she was being held in the Pierce County jail. I couldn't think or speak.

After we hung up, I went into the ladies room where I could be alone. I cried for a long time, in pain for my daughter who was so far away and alone.

I looked up, and asked Why is this happening to my child? Why is this happening to me? When will we have peace?

It seems like there is always one thing after another. Will we ever just be happy?

The next day Scheila called me again and she said "Mom, I got in trouble. I was hanging around with the wrong people, and I did something that was really bad."

Still she didn't tell me what she did. I didn't know what would happen next. In October, she had turned 18 years old—she was an adult now. That December, she went to prison.

I remember I cried almost every day. But then I also prayed every day. I used to say, "God, I know You have a purpose for this girl. I know she's not going to be there for very long."

I believe in God. But at that time, I couldn't understand why things never went easy for me even though I was a strong believer.

I woke up early one morning, at about 3 o'clock. I got up and prayed, asking God to help my daughter. I said, "God, I need to do something. I can't let things stay this way. I have to reach out to her." The answer to what I should do came to me then. I went to our desk and logged onto the computer.

I typed a letter, about 2500 words. I attached that letter to an email to about 100 different churches in Seattle, WA. I asked if somebody could go to the jail and see my daughter and speak *Life* to her.

I needed someone who would encourage her, and build up her confidence that God loves her. She needed to be taught that God would be with her, no matter what happened next.

Scheila didn't want anything to do with God. Every time that I spoke to her she would say, "Your God is not doing anything." She recoiled against anything having to do with God. But I needed her to know that she wasn't alone, that she was loved.

I sent that email and I prayed, "God, whatever you do, I know that You're going to do it for the good of my daughter. I have so much faith!"

Even though it was painful to be her mother and not be able to help, how could I allow myself to give up on my little girl? I couldn't just give up on her. I could never give up.

The next day I went to work, still in pain, and very emotional. My happiness was gone. My joy was gone. I couldn't stop thinking about the things that Scheila must be going through in jail.

When I arrived at work, I saw that my phone had the red message light flashing. I listened to the voice mail. It was a Puerto Rican pastor from Seattle, reaching out to me in response to that 3 AM email.

"I understand what you're going through. My son was also in jail, in the same prison that your daughter is in now. I'm willing to go and visit your daughter this Thursday at 5 o'clock in the afternoon."

God had answered my petition.

He sent me an email the next day after he went to the prison. *I went to see your daughter. She's doing okay.*

He was faithful to his promise to visit her, and, to my relief, he continued to go. Little by little, Scheila started accepting a little bit more. And then he sent me an email that was so special. *I got to speak to Scheila. We read the book of Psalms together.*

I sent Scheila books to read. She has since told me that she never wanted to read those books. All the letters I used to send she would throw right in the garbage. She was very mad at me because she felt like I had let her down.

I understand why she would feel that way. When things were all chaos and confusion with their father, Cheo would hide in his room, so he didn't see or hear a lot. But Scheila was witness to it all. Although I knew that I hadn't, I tried to understand why she felt that I had turned my back on her.

In time, Scheila came to realize that I had always been there for her. She also came to accept that, ultimately, she was responsible for making her own bad choices.

At first, Scheila was not very responsive to the Pastor's visits, but he kept going anyway. Then one glorious day, he emailed me to tell me that Sheila had accepted Jesus Christ as her Lord and Savior.

I can't describe the happiness that I felt at that moment! All I could think was, *Now we'll see—this is going to turn a different way!*

# *Confidence*

Scheila became more accepting of things about me. And she gave permission for the lawyer to speak to me. So one day I spoke to the lawyer.

"John. My name is Sioni. I'm Scheila's Mom. I live in New Jersey. I can't go to see my daughter. She doesn't want me to visit her, but please tell me how you see things are going to go with Scheila's case."

"I'll tell you, Mrs. Rodriguez. Your daughter is facing between 7 and 14 years of jail."

When he said that to me, I felt another knife through my heart. I hung up the phone, not knowing what to think or what to do about this.

Scheila started to change her tone when she spoke to me. She now believed that God was going to help her get out of there. She believed things would turn around and that God had a purpose for her.

On one call the lawyer said, "Tomorrow, I'm going to go see Scheila. We're going to be going to court next week. For what Scheila did, they are offering a plea bargain. They want to give her 7 years instead of 14. I recommend that she take the 7 years.

I said to him, "John, you need to understand, she's not going to be in for 7 years, she's not going to be there for 14. Scheila's going to come out before it's even been a year. As a matter of fact, the day you go to court, my daughter's coming out. I know! I have complete faith. I know, I know, I know."

He couldn't believe what I had just told him. "Do you realize what you're saying? We're not going to win this case. I'm a public defender. I can only give this a limited amount of time. And I don't have the resources that the state has. What your daughter did is a very big thing."

But my faith was strong. I was completely sure that she was going to get out because of our faith. I had gone through so much for a reason. It was to strengthen my faith.

I knew that all this pain, for all these years, all the things that happened to me, were to prepare me for this test. I knew that at some point I was going to be rewarded. There's no way I was going to continue suffering forever. There had to be a point in my life when I would find joy in something good happening. I continued to tell John not to take the plea bargain.

"John. When you go to court, you're not going to be talking alone. God is going to use you to speak His words, and you're going to get my daughter out." He probably thought I was crazy, or at least confused.

Later he relayed our conversation to Scheila.

"Scheila, your mother says you are not to take the plea bargain. She says that you should go to the court, and go through the process because you're going to get out."

And Scheila looked up at the lawyer. "Then do what my mother says."

"But Scheila, you don't understand. If we don't take the plea bargain, we will lose the case. You will go to prison for 14 years."

"Do what my Mom says. My mother is a woman of faith and I believe her that it's going to be okay."

The lawyer called me back. "Listen. I don't know what's wrong with you or your daughter. But if I'm going to court, and we're not taking the plea bargain for your daughter, she's going to be 14 years in prison. And the worst of it is, she told me to do what you say.

"Are you sure Mrs. Rodriguez? Are you sure about this."

"I'm 100% sure. You go ahead with the case in court. You're going to get my daughter out."

The next day was the court date. I remember it was a Wednesday. The court time was 9 AM or noon for us on the east coast. I looked at the clock.

I was positive. "God... You've got this!"

That day I didn't get a phone call from Scheila, and there was no phone call from John.

Nobody called me that day. But I was already done worrying. I that knew God was taking control, so there was no reason for me to be worried about the results at court.

The next day I got the phone call. The display showed the area code.

*253. Okay, this is a Washington state area code.*

I picked up. It was John, the lawyer. He said, "Mrs. Rodriguez?"

I'll never forget this. I've played it over in my mind many times.

"Mrs. Rodriguez. I don't know what God you serve. But whatever God you serve, I want to serve Him too! I have never won a case in my entire career. But I won your daughter's case and she's coming out in two months!"

I was thrilled about my daughter's results! But right now I was completely focused on what he had said about wanting to serve God too. I asked him to repeat this prayer after me

*Jesus,*
*I know now that I have sinned against you. Please forgive me of my sin. Please come into my life and change my heart. I want you to be my Savior. In Jesus name, I pray. Amen.*

He accepted Jesus Christ right then, on that phone call. I couldn't believe it! I was filled with such emotion—this time with joy!

Sheila went to prison in mid-December. And she was released four months later, on April 27. Not after 14 years like the lawyer expected.

Telling the lawyer to go to court instead of taking the plea bargain was one of the boldest things that I've ever done in my life. I was sure. I knew for a fact that Sheila was coming out.

After Scheila was released, she enrolled at a Bible Seminary. Later she got married, and she had a daughter. Scheila has continued in her studies to earn her master's degree in theology and bible study.

I am infinitely proud of her today. I admire her strength, her devotion to family, her self-assurance and her faith. Best of all, she has come to be not only my daughter, but she is also my cherished friend.

As I watch her living her life, growing and living up to her full potential, I am reminded of the lyrics to John Newton's *Amazing Grace...*

*Through many dangers,
toils and snares,
I have already come;
'Tis grace hath brought me
safe thus far,
And grace will lead me home.*

## *Blessing*

While it took Scheila some time to come to Christ, Cheo seems to have always had Him in his heart. Richard introduced the teachings of Christ to Cheo, and he was baptized at the age of 12, the same age when I was baptized. Cheo has been well loved by the congregation at our church.

But like Scheila, he is on his own journey, finding his own way to build his life. So much of what he went through as a boy was a recipe for failure. Yet he was able to overcome it in the most wonderful ways.

When Cheo was a freshman in high school, he wanted to become a lawyer. He has a very logical and organized mind and I could easily see him in a career in the legal system. He was an A+ student and always excelled at his studies.

His teachers and the principal all loved him. They were aware of the problems that he faced growing up, and admired how he had dealt with them. He never exhibited anger towards anyone and never got into trouble.

Cheo conceived a new idea for a group at the school. He went to the principal and suggested that this group would consist of all kids who were from broken homes. They would meet to talk about their challenges and to support one another.

Because of his good standing in the school, the principal gave him permission. The school's guidance counselor was assigned to be the group's advisor.

The group Cheo founded was called *Family Matters*. The kids talked about the problems they had in their homes. They wanted to know from Cheo how he was doing so well in school, even though he had come from such tough circumstances. He spoke of

God to encourage them and to build them up.

Richard suggested that he apply at the United States Military Academy at West Point. He decided to become an engineer and had his sights on the best of the best. I promised I would help him in whatever way I could.

It's quite a long involved process. One of the requirements is to be nominated by a US Senator or State representative. We got all the papers and began the paperwork we would need to complete.

It took a while, but we finally got an appointment with a State Senator. We had an appointment in Edison, NJ to see the State Senator at 10 o'clock on a Saturday morning. We overslept that morning and woke up at 9 o'clock. We only had one hour to dress, prepare and get to Edison. I think the car had wings that day because we actually got there on time. And Cheo got the Senator's nomination.

But nomination didn't guarantee acceptance. Now we had to wait and hope.

Cheo wanted to apply to other schools, just in case. But I said, "No."

I had faith that he would make it. The whole time, we never chased any other college.

Time went by and still they didn't call him.

"Mom, I'm going to go apply at another college."

"No, honey. I know that you're going to get in, I'm sure of it. You're smart and you have a lot to offer that school."

He was concerned because he knew the competition was immense. We didn't have any military connections to give him an edge. He would have to be accepted on his academic record alone. Some months went by and we heard nothing.

I started getting a little anxious and began to doubt that it would happen. It was getting to be the time that the schools were to send out acceptance letters, but his letter didn't come.

Richard and I went on vacation to Costa Rica. Cheo stayed behind to work on what he had to do to finish his senior year. I didn't want to tell Richard how alarmed I was. I didn't want to ruin his vacation, but it was the worst vacation I ever had. I worried through the entire time.

I called home. "Anything in the mail yet, Cheo?"

"No, Mom, nothing in the mail yet."

I called the Captain who was the school recruiter at West Point. He told me, "If they haven't let your son know by this late date, there's a good chance that they're not going to."

I felt my heart break, and I imagined my son's disappointment. I thought, *What am I going to do? I didn't let him apply to any other college!*

I was starting to panic, but I still had the faith that he would be accepted. I didn't say anything during our vacation. We finished our time in Costa Rica and on the last day, I called my son to ask one more time.

"Is there anything in the mail Cheolito?"

"No, Mom. Nothing in the mail."

Our vacation ended and we were on the plane back to the States. I couldn't hold back my emotions any longer. Richard asked me why I was crying. I told him that I was just so sad because Chao hadn't been accepted into West Point. And now it appeared that he would be out a year because it was too late to apply for a good college.

Richard tried to reassure me, "It's going to be fine. He's a smart boy, he'll find a good college." All I could think of was that I had so much hope for him to go to this college. It is one of the best in the world and he deserved the best.

When I got to the airport, Cheo came to pick us up with a neighbor. We were making our way to the baggage claim to get our suitcases, and he was wearing a backpack that said WEST POINT. I didn't pick up on what this implied at first.

"Mom, I wanted to surprise you. I got this a week ago!"

He took off his backpack and took out a piece of paper, and it was his acceptance letter. It said that he had been accepted for the class of 2015. Other than the births of my children, this was one of the happiest moments of my life. I was utterly overjoyed.

Sometimes I look back to when I first came to the United States, and he was playing in his crib as a newborn baby. Back then, I wanted to return to Costa Rica because life here was still too hard. I didn't think there was anything here for *me.*

Then I started to mature as a mother and my focus changed. I began to see that I should not go back to Costa Rica because there was nothing there for *my children.*

There was nothing more important to me than a better future for my children. When Cheo showed me that letter, I fell on the ground and cried like a baby because my dreams were coming true.

"Thank you, God, that I never left. Even though I went through so much here, it's good that I stayed. Otherwise, my son would not have the future that he has today."

It turns out that he didn't need any military connections to get into West Point.

He had all the 'edge' he needed to get in – he had God!

Cheo graduated in 2015. We had a wonderful party for him up at West Point. Everyone came to share this marvelous day. Family from all sides, friends and even my coworkers were there to wish him well. This is such a prestigious school. Only the most select men and women are chosen to attend and there was my little boy graduating among them.

As I watched my son receive his diploma I thought of one of my favorite bible verses:

*For I know the plans I have for you," declares the Lord, "plans to prosper you and not to harm you, plans to give you hope and a future.*

*Jeremiah 29:11*

# Future

Life, as usual, continues to change and rearrange. Now, much to my surprise, I am a grandmother.

Scheila has a little girl. Her name is Xianni, which is my middle name, and she is four years old. I may be biased, but she is just beautiful!

She is very smart and her vocabulary is amazing. Scheila is an incredible mother and Xianni adores her. Xianni is a happy, well-adjusted, confident and calm toddler. All that Scheila has been through has shaped her into a fantastic mother.

Her husband, Khalil is very kind and loving man. He is a good husband and an involved dad. When they visit it is so wonderful to watch him help Scheila.

They had a beautiful outdoor, summer wedding. It was a clear, shining, sunlit day. Scheila had chosen red and white as her colors. Everything just shone like jewelry in the bright sunlight. Once again we were joined by family from all sides, good friends and coworkers. What a happy day that was for me. The past had changed into a bright and shining future.

When she got pregnant, Scheila told me she was nervous about it. I thought it was going to be hard for her, but she's a better mother than I was. She has a full-time job, and she goes to school full time. She's amazing. Scheila is not who she once was. Sometimes I look at her and I am amazed at how someone can change so much. It's like night and day. She's a very good daughter and a very good mom.

One day we were talking about what it is like to raise a child and she said to me, "Mom, I promise you that I will never, ever mess up. I will never let you down where this baby is concerned. This is a gift from God and I am always going to do the right thing for my daughter.

I love my granddaughter and she's very precious to me. When she visits we do lots of things together. We watch a movie together; we play together. It's so much fun to be with her. The best thing about it is, as with all grandchildren, she goes back to her mom when I'm exhausted.

Scheila says, "Mom you damaged my daughter. You've spoiled her!"

"God commanded us, "Thou shalt spoil thy grandchildren completely.' It's the eleventh commandment!"

Xianni has given me back the time that I couldn't spend with my children because I was so busy with work. It was all I could do to hold myself together. Now she has awakened that place in my heart that allows me to be young and playful and to enjoy our time together.

I was there when Xianni was born. What an incredible moment the birth of your child's child, like watching yourself be reborn. Two weeks later, when I was visiting Scheila, she looked at me and said, "You know, Mom, I'm so sorry for everything I did to you."

In the past, she had apologized. But now after the baby was born she looked at me with such love and kindness. She said, "Mom, I'm so sorry I was such a spoiled brat. Please forgive me. I did such bad things to you. But now I'm a mom, and I realize how hard you must have had it. I love you."

My heart was so full to hear her say this. I said, "Scheila, I love you too. It's all done and past and there's nothing to forgive. I love you so much and that baby has made me special again."

Cheo met his future wife when they were both attending West Point. They were friends back then, but didn't date. After graduation Cheo was stationed in Korea. When he returned to the States, he was sent to Oklahoma. Maya was there too. They renewed their friendship and soon they were dating. Not long after, they were engaged, married, and living in California.

Last December, a couple of days before Cheo's birthday, Sergio was born. Like his dad, he is a Christmas baby and a joyous gift to our family.

Richard and I went to meet my son's wife and baby in the spring. It was breathtaking to see them together. She's a woman of God, very humble, and very smart. She's loving and caring.

The baby is amazing! We were blown away by the how beautifully they were taking care of their baby. This pair of Army 2nd Lieutenants are doing things to ensure the well-being of their child that I never did!

Cheo is such a man of integrity and character. I know my little grandson will be given all the right tools for a happy and successful life. Cheo has a tender heart balanced by tremendous courage. I can't wait to see how he raises his son.

I always prayed for a Godly husband and wife for my children. I prayed that they would each find a good spouse. We've been very blessed with both. Khalil is an excellent husband and father. Maya is a good wife and mom; beautiful, both inside and out. The four of them are excellent parents to our grandchildren. And now they have become close as sisters and brothers.

My family is growing and my blessings are increasing. If everything I endured was necessary so that my family would flourish, it was well worth all that I went through.

## *Peace In God*

I have chosen to forget about all of the bad things that my ex-husband did to me. That's in the past. I feel it is more important to live in the present and look to the future.

He is very much a part of Scheila's and Cheo's lives now. He is good to his grandchildren, and he is as involved as possible with them. He probably feels guilty about everything, so that now he wants to give it all he's capable of.

Scheila led him to Christ a while ago. And he asked for my forgiveness. But I had already made the decision to forgive him. I could see that he had become supportive of the children. He wanted to share in all their important milestones.

At first it was understandably hard for Richard to accept that I forgave my ex-husband. Richard was angry on my behalf because of what I had suffered.

But Richard is a good man, and he realized how important it was for me to let go of the past. The choice to forgive was a gift to my ex-husband. It was also a gift to myself so that I could be released from the anger and the hurt. Beyond that, Richard knew how important my forgiveness was for the children to begin to heal.

It helped that I never told the kids anything about what was happening to me. Scheila saw what she saw, but I never poisoned their minds about their father.

I didn't tell them the full story until Cheo was 18 and Scheila was 20. Now that they're adults they were able to accept it for what it was. They have a good relationship with their father, which is the best thing for all of us. They have made the right choice to have a loving relationship with their father.

When Scheila got married, she wanted both her father and Richard to walk her down the aisle. When they gave her to be married, they both kissed Scheila, one on each side. It was a very sweet and special gesture for her wedding day.

It was the same when my son graduated from West Point. Richard was on one side, and his father on the other side as he became an officer. Richard deserved to be a part of these occasions. The children love Richard and he is always there for them. They call him "Papi" or "Pops."

How did we change from having a tough relationship to a great marriage? Decisions, decisions! We made the decision to make our marriage work. We kept our relationship with God as the central focal point in our marriage. In my entire life, my happiest years have been in the present.

My children are both married to good spouses. I am blessed to be a grandmother. Richard and I are starting to plan our retirement. I have the opportunity to speak *Life* to others and I grow closer to the Lord every day.

Now that it's just Richard and me at home, we are closer than ever. Now we can meet somewhere without having to worry about coming home because the kids are waiting. We are intimate and we're very close. We both have a strong relationship with God, and this has made everything better.

We have our problems, but it's quite different now. The way we deal with our differences now is very healthy. There's much less stress. And I've learned to choose my battles! We're married, but we're good friends too.

And we never go to a hamburger joint to make up any more like on our first date. No more dollar menus for our dates now!

I have had it in my heart since I was a young girl to do God's work. The moment I walked into that little house across from the grocery in Oriente, I felt His presence was real. Since then, I've wanted to speak His words. Along the way there have been some detours, but I am doing now what I always knew I should be doing.

There's been *much* healing in our lives. It feels like God gave me back everything the devil wanted to take away from me. And He's given me a double portion of everything good!

*After Job had prayed for his friends, the Lord restored his fortunes and gave him twice as much as he had before.*

*Job 42:10*

# *Belief*

I believe that when Jesus saved me, he did it for a reason. I use all that I experienced and all that I know of suffering to help others wherever I can. I think that God requires this from all of us. Whatever our life events have been, I believe God expects us to use the experience to aid and comfort others.

I focus my life on bringing the comfort and strength of our Savior to those in the midst of pain and hardship. I volunteer in a prison ministry through our church. I am a member of a ministry that fights against human trafficking. I also speak out against domestic abuse, and work with the wonderful people at *Angel Tree.* But the first two ministries are my primary callings.

The prison ministry is very dear to me. In fact, I love going to the prison! I know that must sound odd. Obviously, it's not the prison that I love. It's the opportunity to bring hope that inspires me.

Time passes so fast when we're there. Richard goes to the male section, while I go to the female side. Once or twice a month, we'll go to maximum security. Sometimes the prisoners don't want to hear our message, and I understand that. But there are others who are willing and anxious to receive. I can tell when they sincerely want to change.

I bring the word of God to the inmates. Like the Puerto Rican pastor who helped me, I tell them that I understand because my daughter was a prisoner too.

I love to speak *Life* to people. I tell them how, with faith and love, people can survive, get strong and live up to their full potential. I've seen that people can and do change. God gives us second chances. I tell them not to dwell on the past, but instead to move on with life in the present.

# Belief

Sometimes, women don't want to hear this message. I understand that. God has a purpose for each of us, but we get to choose what we'll do. I let them know that I don't judge. But I also make it clear that nothing will ever separate them from the love of God, no matter what they've done.

These women have done wrong and made bad decisions. I have empathy for them. Many of them have had the worst upbringing, as I did. They didn't think they had any choice but to do what they did.

I want them to know that God can make good from any mess. He'll help them and love them, just as they are.

I remind them that they don't have to make this prison their home. It's only a place they are passing through. Better things are in store if they make the right choices.

I bring the Word of God to these women. I show them that there is a better way. I share with them the words of comfort and hope that are His words. I tell them that it's possible to move ahead into a bright future. I explain that what I say is real and true. I know because I've lived it.

I'm one of the teachers at the prison. Every eight months there is a graduation. It's so encouraging to hear what they have to say! They might not believe in God when they start the program. But at the end, they will have learned the truth about Jesus.

I also learn from the inmates. Here's an example of how learning comes to me as well.

Sometimes I go the next week and learn that a girl has been released. Sometimes we'll find out that she overdosed and died on the outside. Three girls that I became close to in the past two years have died this way. I've looked in their eyes and told them how beautiful they were. That God had great things in their lives and God had a purpose for them. I told them, "You're not here on this earth just to take up space. You're here to do something. To make a difference."

And then the next thing I know, they're gone.

The first time this happened was in 2014. I was preparing to go to Puerto Rico. One of the girls told me that she was being released. I had been teaching this girl for almost two years.

I asked her what she was going to do when she got out. She came up with a list and she told about her plans. I was so excited for her, told her that it all sounded amazing, and asked her to call me. I suggested that we could go to church together.

When I returned from my trip, I went to the prison. The girls were unusually quiet, but I didn't know why. I asked if they knew what happened to her. "I'm waiting for her to call, but she hasn't called me yet."

They told me, "Sioni, you haven't heard the news. Well, she died. She overdosed."

The girls took it hard, after all the time they had spent together. They told me she had only been out of prison for eight days when she overdosed. I was completely saddened, thinking of the plans that would never happen now.

That was the first time that I thought this might not be the right work for me. I questioned what I was doing there. I questioned if I was doing any good at all. I asked one of the girls what she thought about my misgivings, and here's what she told me.

"We all have to make choices. Sometimes we make the right choices, and sometimes bad choices. It has nothing to do with you, Sioni. It has to do with us as individuals."

Her statement helped me to understand. I can teach a better way to someone, but that person has to have a willingness to change. We can't change people. That's not my job. Only they can change themselves.

Now I recognize that my job is to encourage and teach how God loves us all. That God is their father who doesn't give up on them.

On occasion, I'll run into a girl who was a former inmate. I might be in the grocery store and there'll be one of them, out in the world working, and making her way. I'm blessed when I know they're doing well.

***...whoever refreshes others will be refreshed.***

***Proverbs 11:25***

As much as I love witnessing at the prison, the fight against human trafficking is my true passion. I speak at conferences and churches whenever and wherever I'm asked. I want to inform as many people as possible about this insidious evil.

The problem is not only in third world countries. People in this country need to know that it is here too. I want to make people aware and angry. Everyone, even our own families could be at risk.

The group I work with teaches awareness, prevention, and protection. You don't have to be a Christian to receive help, but you might become one while you're with us.

Being a human trafficking survivor is not easy. Many programs for these survivors can afford to give them only a short amount of time in a protected home. There aren't enough resources to cover the need. When their time is over, they are often out on their own again. And the perpetrators are waiting to get their victims back.

The Super Bowl is one of the largest venues for human trafficking in America. Thousands of men with money, come together in a major city for this day. This creates a market for traffickers. Money, alcohol, and drugs... the perfect ingredients to feed this monster.

Every year, I try to go to the city where the Super Bowl is being held with other volunteers who are committed to fighting human trafficking. We move throughout the host city with the goal of bringing awareness to as many people as possible. We hand out leaflets, flyers, and photos of missing children given to us by law enforcement. In order to reach the most travelers, we make a point to be at the airports, train stations, and the bus stops. Much of the time is spent talking to the crowds outside the stadium as they gather to see what our group is all about.

Last year, I was with a group of volunteers who drove around the city, looking for girls and boys who may need to be rescued. For the years when I'm unable to go to the game city in person, I make it a day of prayer.

I have experienced sexual, verbal, physical and domestic abuse. I survived the exploitation and the ordeal of having been trafficked. Because of this, it is my deepest passion to bring healing to others who have been victimized, as I was. I know firsthand how suffering these traumas can completely unravel someone's life. I have been in that place of emotional despair, isolation and misery.

A dream of mine is to build a ministry that provides shelter and safety for survivors for as long as they need. It would become a haven where they can restore themselves and begin again. It should be a place where they can heal not only in body but in spirit as well. In this place, they will hear of the hope and love that God's grace provides. They will have an opportunity to begin again.

*Therefore, if anyone is in Christ, he is a new creation: the old has gone, the new has come!*

*2 Corinthians 5:17*

# *Thankful*

Most people would look at my childhood in horror. They would expect—with all the misery I endured—that I was destined for a meaningless life.

Yet, here I am today. My life is the complete opposite of what it seemed sure to be back then. It is full, challenging, fulfilling and peaceful.

I have been saved by the grace of God. I want others who have suffered to find that same peace. To find that beauty in life that we can all have if we have Jesus in our lives.

God knows my heart, and the reasons why I've written this book. I write to encourage as many people as I can reach.

What I want you to know is that even when we think there's no way, it turns out that there is a way. When we think that we're alone, we're not, because God is with us. Sometimes we feel worthless, and think that God must not care about people like us. That's not so either.

We are His precious children, and He loves us more than we can ever understand.

Sometimes I look back over my life and I pray,

*Thank you, Lord,*
*because you have made me, and then molded me into what you want. Thank you for giving me the strength I needed to go through the all the things the devil used to try to destroy me.*

Everything that the devil made to be evil, God turned around and made to be beautiful. Any good that has come of my life is not for my personal gain, but all to show the glory of God. Even though it seemed like God wasn't in the picture, He was there with me, and loving me all along.

The Bible includes a book of ancient scripture called Esther. Surprisingly, God is not mentioned once. But His fingerprints are all over the pages. It's plain to see the perfect timing of the fortunate events that made the deliverance of the Jews possible. It's clear that God was working to protect His people.

That's how it was in my life. It didn't seem like God was with me, but He was behind the scenes the whole time. God was the one who made things right for me. It was never in my own power.

He kept me alive, even those times when I was ready to take my own life. He used the evil done to me when I was sold the third time, as a conduit for getting me out from under my mother's control. To give me courage along the way, He put Abuela Lili and the little church family in my life. Surely, He was with me every day.

Brokenness can come from terrible experiences in our lives. But as terrible as these times of brokenness can be, God is able to heal and restore us.

I survived so that I could tell people that forgiveness is the most beautiful gift that you can give to someone. And that it's possible to give the gift of forgiveness to yourself.

I can be trusted to know that it is possible for us to forgive—even after unspeakable torment—because I've done it myself. I am living proof that what the devil meant to destroy, God can turn around for good, because He did this for me. And He promises that He will do the same for you when you accept Him into your life.

*Father God, allow our lives to demonstrate how You will never abandon us. Let the world know peace through Your Saving Grace!*

# ABOUT THE AUTHOR

Sioni Rodriguez is a fierce advocate for victims of human trafficking, domestic violence, and sexual assault. Her goal is to both raise awareness, and to instill hope—hope in knowing they can move from "survivor" status to living peaceful and fulfilling lives. She knows they can, because she's done it herself!

Sioni has joined with the *A Time to Heal, Beyond Survival International Ministry Team*, which was founded by Rev. Sue Willis. This International Ministry offers hope and healing for people who have suffered from the trauma of rape, sexual assault, or are survivors of trafficking.

Sioni and her husband, Richard Rodriguez, are fully engaged in the prison ministry of their home church in Pennsylvania, and in other ministries that help people in need and at risk. Another mission that's close to their hearts is to spend time enjoying their family and friends.

*Sioni can be reached by email at srwestpointmom@gmail.com.*

CPSIA information can be obtained
at www.ICGtesting.com
Printed in the USA
BVOW09s1946251117
501251BV00023B/944/P